Behind the Smile

Emma Pearson

to have complete control over their finished book whilst utilising the expert advice and services usually reserved for traditionally published print, in order to produce an attractive, engaging, quality product. Please note, however, that final editorial decisions and approval rests with the author.

ISBN 978-1-9164415-2-1

Printed in the U.K.

ALL PROFITS FROM THE BOOK WILL BE DONATED TO THE CHARITY

'JOEL – THE COMPLETE PACKAGE'.

Dedication

This book is dedicated to...

Noel and James Pearson, our twin sons, born beautiful but still at 26 weeks in 2011. How I have spent every day dreaming of you and what you both could have been. You changed our lives forever, and you are loved and missed more every day.

Sebastian and Polly Pearson, our rainbows, our hope and our life. You are beautiful and beyond precious. Always be true to yourself, never let anyone dull your spirit and do what makes your heart happy, as you certainly make my heart burst with love, pride, and happiness. You are my heart.

My husband Matt, my best friend, my rock and my soul mate. Not only do you deserve a medal for your tolerance in allowing a charity to take over my life and our entire house, but you are ace, and I am so proud of you. *"Whether times are good or bad, happy or sad."**

*Al Jackson Jr / Willie Mitchell / Al Green- Let's Stay Together

To my mum and dad, thank for being the only people to buy my book. Just kidding! You really are the best and thank you for bringing me up to never lose my character, for your love and support and for celebrating the lives of ALL your grandchildren.

For my friends and family – some of you feature in this book. I am so grateful for your love and support.

For the families who have experienced their own loss and heartache: you inspire me every single day, and I am so proud to know about you and your children.

Love you all!

CONTENTS

Say what you want

Break my heart a thousand times

James Dean Bradfield, Manic Street Preachers- Distant Colours

INTRODUCTION

Where to start.......

Someone (well, a couple of people) in the past have told me, "Emma, you're strong, you can cope", as though it is a badge of honour that I don't crumble in front of people when they say something to me that is upsetting. It's like you just have to take it on the chin, but that doesn't work both ways, and I would never be able to say anything back in return.

Yes, I am a strong person. Yes, I may appear to have confidence, but who says that it's not just a front? Isn't it judgmental to treat or speak to people in different ways because of how they could react or, in effect, 'cope' with it? Think about people you know who you think can 'cope with it' and wonder what is happening behind their eyes, within their heart, and in their soul.

Who says being strong and coping is the right way to deal with anything? Occasionally, if one of my children trips and falls the other child will say, "were you brave?" or, "did you cry?" I don't know where it comes from as it is something we would never say but who says it's brave not to cry? It isn't any wonder that men (in particular) struggle with this as the ridiculous perception of being a man is to be strong – usually on behalf of someone else – to bury their own feelings until they can't any longer, with their mental health suffering dreadfully, sometimes with tragic consequences. And this could really resonate in the story I am going to share with you. I can't imagine having to feel as though I have to hold everything together and not express my own emotions. It is definitely more readily accepted that women can be more open and have a louder voice about mental health and how they feel (although this still needs to improve too).

Who knows if people who appear to be strong cry themselves to sleep each night or have a mind full of worry and anxiety?

There is no right or wrong way to deal with anything; who are we to decide when and how someone should be feeling? Sometimes things are going swimmingly, and then something can happen to change you and your life forever totally.

We are all individuals, we look and feel in different ways at different times, making us the incredible people that we are. We need to embrace who we are and how we feel and stop living our lives in a box created by others and using benchmarks of how others felt at particular times. This can make us unhappy, make us feel as though we don't 'fit in', and increase our anxiety.

We all have our story to tell: stories filled with happy times and stores filled with heartache. This is mine.

Don't ever forget that being you, being true to yourself and making time for you is super important, after all; you are bloody ace!

As my memory rests

But never forgets what I lost

Wake me up when September ends

Michael Pritchard / Frank E. / Iii Wright / Billie Joe Armstrong, Green

Day- Wake me up when September Ends

Chapter 1

Loved with a love beyond all feeling

Friday 9th September 2011.

I went to work and was in class for most of the day. I felt great and was really feeling positive about my pregnancy. I was excited to answer all the questions my students had about being pregnant and the prospect of being a mummy to twins. My bump was huge and had grown a lot over the past few days and was really itchy as it just felt so tight. I must have been having a growth spurt. I had been for a scan two days previously, and everything looked well, except the sonographer had noticed a tiny difference in amniotic fluid levels between twin one and twin two. It was nothing significant, but it was picked up, and we were grateful for a keen eye during the scan. Each scan was followed by a consultant appointment; we had both regularly as our twins were mono-chorionic di-amniotic and this meant they shared the same placenta but had a membrane separating them both.

I always joked I would have twins; my grandma's brother and sister were twins so they ran in the family and I kind of half expected it. Apparently, they are more common in women who are over thirty and tall (I am not sure that it's completely true I remember reading it somewhere), but as I'm just over six foot tall and I was 29 years old when pregnant with my twins, it kind of made sense.

The consultant explained that we would now be scanned every two weeks instead of every four and if things continued to change we would be referred to Jessops in Sheffield as they would be able to give us specialist care. We were also warned of the possibility that if we went back for further scans and there were huge changes that we would have to prepare for an emergency delivery that day. Now I know this sounds dramatic, but at the time we felt calm, and we weren't scared. We took it all in our stride and knew we were in safe hands. After all, I was past the 24-week benchmark, and everyone knows that twins are notorious for arriving early. I expected to get to about 30 weeks and just keep plodding; they were both growing well and wriggling away so what more could I ask? If we were given any further advice, I can't remember it; no monitoring of movements, no explanation that it could be twin-to-twin transfusion syndrome (TTTS), no warning that suddenly I would start to experience the worst pain ever – which was a huge warning sign – but who would know that?

When I discovered I was pregnant with twins, I did some research and came across Tamba (the Twin and Multiple Birth Association) and read a small amount about TTTS. I recall thinking that surely that kind of stuff doesn't happen now. The information was brief, and I read it, but I can't remember much more than that.

I finished work on the Friday and went straight over to my mum and dad's house for tea. My husband was away in Cornwall on a stag do for the weekend. I stood up, and as I did, something just felt different, it was like my back just went. I can't describe it really, but it was just such a significant moment. My mum could tell by my face that something had happened, but the babies were still moving away, and my bump was huge, so I expected it was the usual pregnancy issues. I had a load of problems with my pelvis when pregnant and wore a support band; perhaps it was a long day at work taking its toll.

I went to bed that night and I couldn't sleep. I felt really uncomfortable. The next day my friend Rochelle came to visit from London, and we had a lovely girly evening and catch up – just what I needed. I couldn't get comfy though, and no matter how I sat or laid, it was painful. I couldn't wait for Matt to come home but I gave myself a good talking to and just kept going.

By Sunday Matt was home – thank goodness. By that evening I was in agony and totally exhausted. I must have had four hours sleep over three nights, and now I was getting really worried. At about 5am I phoned the labour ward, and even though they assured me I would be okay, I went up to be checked. The midwife thought I had a water infection, which made sense with the pain, but every test she did came back negative, so she took a sample that could be sent away and examined properly, just in case anything was being missed. I was attached to a monitor and everything was good. I wish I had mentioned that I was losing a tiny bit of fluid at different parts of the day, but I didn't realise that's what it was and felt embarrassed as I thought it was how the twins were laid on my bladder. I was sent away and told to lie over a gym ball or bean bag as probably the weight of my bump was causing the problem and if there were any other issues to go back. I cried, a lot. How could I put up with this pain for what could be potentially another ten weeks? I am no wimp, but I was in agony and knackered.

The week was awful, but my dad, bless him, was a legend and kept coming to see me in the day. I remember so clearly him picking me up to drive me to the Asda just around the corner from where we lived. The pain of just sitting in the car was unbearable and whilst walking around the shop I just burst out crying. I could hardly walk, and the pain was horrific, my pelvis felt as though it was being broken into a thousand pieces and surely that was not normal.

Wednesday 14ᵗʰ September 2011

I phoned the chiropractor and asked for advice, and they agreed to see me. My dad took me there, and after the treatment I felt slightly better, thinking perhaps I wouldn't have to try and sleep for another night on a dining table chair back to front with my forehead resting on a pillow placed on the backrest.

We visited the hospital for an antenatal class on a water birth but were told when we got there that it wouldn't be possible for twins. I couldn't sit still, and I was in so much pain, the plastic chairs we sat on didn't help. I had to keep leaving the room to pace the corridors, and the lady delivering the session came to see if I was okay. I was propped up and leaning over a stand trying to relieve my back and explained I'd been having trouble with my pelvis.

Thursday 15ᵗʰ September 2011

I felt slightly better; it was a miracle! I could move more, and I wasn't just restricted to the settee and a million cushions, *hurrah*.

I sat on the settee in my dressing gown and drank a

huge glass of cold lemonade. The twin on my right started kicking and moving like crazy, I hadn't felt movement like that before. I texted Matt to say that our boys were having a good wiggle, it was nice as they had been quite quiet for the previous few days.

I wanted to make the most of feeling better, and the lovely sunshine so decided to spend the day sorting through the twins' clothes and washing them in preparation. If they were going to come early then, we needed to be prepared. I had a line filled with beautiful white babygrows and blankets, and I was visited by my best friend Ruth and her gorgeous six-month-old son Flynn. I could not believe how good I felt, it was incredible.

We were sat having a natter when my phone rang. I stood up to get the phone from the fireplace, and as I stood up, I thought my waters had broken. Oh shit! It was Matt calling me, and I told him what had just happened. I phoned my midwife who told me to call the labour ward immediately and they told me to pop to the ward and be checked over. I just remember crying and not knowing what to do; I couldn't drive because of the pain, so I called my dad to pick me up and phoned Matt to ask him to meet me at the hospital. I knew it would be a while before Matt arrived as his work wasn't that close by. This all must have happened around 3.30pm as when I called my dad he was picking my mum up from work at school and they came straight over to take me to the hospital.

I remember being sat at the traffic lights not far from where we lived, and everything around me just looked different. I was terrified. I knew I was going to the hospital for them to hopefully stop or delay my labour and knew that our boys would be on the special care baby unit fighting for their lives. It would be a fight, but we could do it and we would. It was such a surreal moment, and I can remember it clear as day.

We got to the hospital and after Matt arrived my mum and dad left us to be alone. I was being hooked up to a monitoring machine, but I couldn't lay still, the pain was too bad. My tummy was so huge now that my skin was virtually transparent and the left-hand side of my bump was the biggest it had been for a couple of days. The monitor was placed on my tummy on the left-hand side; this is where Noel lay with his head down and his bum under my ribs. There was nothing, but he did like to hide, and we had experienced many times where it had taken a while to find his heartbeat. I wasn't worried. They placed the monitor on my right side, the side where James lay in a breach position, and there was a heartbeat. The midwife kept us calm and just said that she was going to get a consultant to check the location of the twins so she could monitor us correctly, and then give me steroids to help their lungs develop.

The consultant came with the scanner and quietly took everything in. I remember just chatting to Matt, oblivious and not even contemplating what we were about to be told. "I am sorry, I can't appreciate a heartbeat". Okay, what have you just said, what do you appreciate? I didn't understand what she meant. "Can you say it again please?" "Your babies have died, there is no heartbeat". I opened my mouth to scream, but nothing came out. I felt like I was choking on my tears and I looked over to Matt, and I will never ever forget the look on his face. I think I apologised to him, I had let him down, I had let our boys down, and I felt sick with disgust for myself. My heart shattered into a thousand pieces and time stood still. All I could hear was the couple next to us behind a curtain and the sound of their baby's heart beating away on the monitor.

I have no idea how, but Matt called our parents to tell them their grandchildren had died. I had to be taken to the sonography department, which luckily had just closed at 5pm, so there was the small mercy that I didn't have to be faced with a waiting room full of pregnant women. I don't know how I walked there. I just remember wailing down the corridor and thinking I was going to be sick or just collapse. I thought I was going to have to crawl there on my hands and knees. We were taken into one of the rooms and the consultant started scanning my tummy. I looked at the screen, praying it was all a huge mistake, only to see two lifeless, slumped bodies on their sides. It felt like a nightmare, and I was sure I was going to wake up at any moment.

What the hell had just happened to us, we didn't deserve this? What had we ever done to deserve this?

On and off from that moment, it all blurs into one, and there are so many things I can and can't remember. We were taken to a labour room where I was examined, and both sets of parents waited outside. I had already started to dilate, so I ran a bath and laid there with my mum sat on the side of the bath. I laid and looked at my bump and how I wish I had savoured that moment instead of the disgust I felt for myself. I asked for pain relief as the contractions started and remember our families just staring at me. I remember having too much gas and air and laughing, actually laughing, in the midst of it all.

We texted all our friends and told them. It was nighttime, just me and Matt and a wonderful midwife. I was off my chops with morphine (how I wish I hadn't had this) but it did actually help me sleep, the first time in over a week. I woke in the morning to be greeted by three lovely midwives, one of them a student, and by this point, my contractions were coming thick and fast. I remember seeing my mum and dad and looking at their faces; I can't imagine what it must have been like for them, seeing their daughter like that and losing their grandchildren all at the same time.

I remember my mum telling them to break my waters, and when they did, they went with such force it made me move on the bed. We went through our options. We knew Noel would be born first and the midwives asked if we wanted him to be placed on my chest or in a Moses basket. I chose the Moses basket as I was too scared knowing I would have to give birth again whilst cuddling my first born. I didn't know if I would have the strength to do it twice.

Noel was born at 10.34am; I glanced down and saw him on the bed before he was moved, but I was too scared to look. Noel was followed by his brother James who was born at 12.15pm. The midwives were just incredible, and we owe them so much for the care and support we received at this time. Our boys were wrapped in blankets and brought over to us; Noel was given to Matt, and James to me. I was absolutely terrified to hold them and look at their beautiful faces. I knew seeing them would make me love them more and make it even harder to say goodbye; I knew as soon as I started cuddling them that I would never ever want to let them go.

As I was holding James, my contractions started again, and I screamed for the midwives to take him from me. My placenta had broken up into pieces which resulted in part of it being removed manually. I remember looking around and seeing the room full of consultants, doctors, and midwives; I remember looking at the sheer horror on Matt's face.

After things settled, our parents and our brothers came in to meet Noel and James, they held them and cried. Our boys were simply beautiful.

From this point onwards, I can't really remember what happened. Did I hold Noel and James again? I don't know. Did I kiss them? I can't remember, although I remember the sensation of their skin on my lips so I must have. We were moved to Birth Room 5, my mum and dad came to visit, along with my friend Ruth. Our boys weren't in the room then. I'm not sure where they were – maybe that's when they were taking the hand and footprints and dressing them in clothes we had to use from the Special Care Baby Unit as nothing we had would fit their long but skinny 2lb bodies.

Our boys were later brought into our room dressed. I remember holding them both together, and we have such a beautiful photo from this moment. The chaplain came to bless them and then we chose to say goodbye. Their skin was fragile, and the room was so hot. We wanted to remember them exactly how they looked – asleep. So we said both our hellos and our goodbyes on the 16th September 2011.

We left the hospital the next morning, my mum and dad taking us home. I made everyone at the hospital promise the boys would stay together and that they would never be separated. They had always been together, and we never wanted them to be alone. I remember driving away from the hospital with empty arms and a broken heart. I felt like the world had ended even though looking around everyone just seemed to be carrying on with their normal lives. How could they? How did they not know our lives had just fallen apart? Noel and James died because of 'Twin to Twin Transfusion Syndrome'. We were told at the hospital that it was clear something wasn't right, and it was confirmed via the post-mortem results by my consultant six weeks later. Abnormal blood vessel connections form in the placenta, resulting in one twin receiving more amniotic fluid, blood and other nutrients than the other. Usually, the recipient-donor is the one that dies first as their heart can't cope with the volume of blood, and this was Noel. This makes sense as to why my bump bulged on the side where he lay. James was severely anaemic; I still remember the morning my waters broke and how he was wriggling in a completely different way, this was the last movement I felt, and I tortured myself for a long time about those movements being James fighting for his life.

So, having left the hospital and going back into the big wide world we had absolutely no idea of what we would do from this point onwards. Here began our journey and our life after loss.

I should be crying but I just can't let it show

I should be hoping but I can't stop thinking

Kate Bush- Woman's Work

Chapter 2

Chasing Rainbows

After the loss of a baby or babies, your life changes forever in so many different ways. I can't seem to remember 'me' prior to 2011, and I spent so long wanting to be that person I once was, but without ever really knowing who that person was anymore. I just wanted to feel (get ready!) normal! What is normal anyway?! Whatever normal is, I don't think I have ever been it.

Let me take you back to the 'old' me. I was born in Worksop in the early 80's, and I still live there now. I grew up with my mum, dad and younger (yes I know he looks older than me) brother, Andrew. My mum and dad's house is a lovely 1930's semi-detached house, which was bought as a new build by my great grandparents and is full of family memories and sentiment. I am the second most sentimental person in the world, the first being my mum and therefore love that my family home growing up is still where my parents live today. A care-free and easy-peasy childhood, I know that I am lucky. At primary school, I was a full-on nerd and bookworm, and I loved being there with my friends, many I still keep in touch with now. I got 100% in everything (other than sport, yuck!) and spent my childhood dreaming of being a librarian and surrounded by rooms of beloved books, what a dream. It was such a dream that I even used it to create the little date labels, and tag pockets like you used to get in libraries back in the day and force my poor brother to take them out. I still have these books now, just to remind me that I have always been a bit sad.

By the time I had finished my first year at comprehensive school my rebellious side had kicked in, much to my parent's delight. From then on, my wardrobe became an array of black clothing, my bedroom was painted floor to ceiling in black and resembled a cave, and my face was beyond pale. I only really had a couple of friends at school as we were all branded with the 'mosher' label. I spent my days listening to immature people singing "I want to be a hippy" and loads of other pathetic crap at me all day. I liked what I wore, I liked what my friends wore, and I loved listening to music. I still never understand how people can judge you for how you dress- especially ones that wore Eclipse jeans, but basically, that was the epitome of my teenage years. Halfway through school I started going out, and my friends were older, most probably in a band and school just didn't interest me at all. Now I love learning, don't get me wrong but the break/lunchtime, walking to and from school never felt that great. At least I stood out I suppose, six foot tall, lanky, black hair and para boots probably meant that I looked like Olive Oyl and everyone can remember me from school.

How I loved going out and still do, but at least I don't come home now to my dad sat on the front wall waiting for me because I am hours later home than I should have been.

My dream of being a librarian was squashed by the dream that I should probably be in a band such as

L7 or Babes in Toyland. It then changed to the idea
of working in fashion (there was seriously nowhere
to buy clothes for giants in the 90's!), but instead,
I set upon my quest to become a Make-Up Artist
after leaving school. I was advised to study Beauty
Therapy first, which I did and loved it. I couldn't
imagine doing anything else. Who wouldn't want
to receive a facial from someone who had lightened
their foundation with white face paint, only wore
black eyeshadow and was more than likely wearing
blue lipstick. I wish I had photos of this time, but
they are few and far between, lucky me!

After my college years, I decided to tone it down very
slightly and set up my own salon. I'd trained and
worked hard, loved my industry and just wanted to
make people feel good about themselves. Although,
who knows how I used to manage in the Salon on a
Saturday after two nights on the bounce, no sleep
and one eye on Saturday night. Thank goodness my
hangovers aren't as horrific as they are now - I mean
the headache is bad but the heartburn - Christ! It's
a whole new level.

After a while, I went into teaching, and a few days

into my second teaching job, I walked into a very dashing looking man. Now don't get me wrong, I love working in Beauty Therapy but it was a very female orientated industry, and after about a year of being single and loving it, my dad kept telling me I was never going to meet anyone just working in a small beauty college filled with women. Who cared about that, I was out constantly, spent my whole wages on clothes, socialising, and music and I was happy. I'd always been happy on my own.

Anyway, a few days into my new job, I clapped eyes on Matt. He was totally different to anyone I had been out with before but as cheesy as it sounds the moment I saw him - I knew that was it. A few months later on a stereotypical work's Christmas night out, we got chatting (there is no way I can repeat what he said to me!) but I heard him say he had a girlfriend and flirting aside, I knew that was the end of that. Much to my joy, the said girlfriend was no more just after Christmas, and by the end of January, we were on our first date. What a year it was, it took Matt nine months to sell his house and the fiasco that goes along with it, but we knew if we could stick it through that, we'd do all right.

We bought our house a year after we met and were engaged a few months later (even though we'd already booked our wedding without telling anyone) and our house was the home of 'the' party and what parties we had - every weekend! We used to joke that our house was Pearson's B&B because there was at least one person stopping there every weekend. Matt shared my love for a good time, a bit of mischief and a good drink. What's not to love?

We got married in 2009 after being together for three years and decided that the following year we would try for a family. However, I had important bridesmaid duties to uphold in 2010 followed by some very dodgy cells on my cervix which meant I had to have an operation and hold off the babies for another six months. Up to this point in my adult life, I'd focussed on not getting pregnant, but then it was a whole new game altogether as we tried to make a baby.

Before the moment that changed my life forever, I was a lecturer at an FE college, teaching Beauty Therapy and even though sometimes it drove me to despair I loved it. It was busy, chaotic at times, and fun. Anyone who knows me will know that I get bored very easily – I love to be kept busy and my mind to be stimulated – teaching is very good at doing all this. Our weekends were jam-packed socialising with family and friends and looking back I was so naïve and was innocent to the harsh realities of life. Even writing this now feels like I'm describing a totally different person, it's so surreal.

This is my story of how I kept going during my journey through life after loss.

* * * *

We all experience something in our lives that will change us forever; sometimes it will be for the better and sometimes for the worse. When it's for the worse, you have the choice to either give up or somehow you keep going. In the first few months, my life felt like a huge black hole that I had no control of whatsoever.

Things that used to be easy and that were part of an everyday routine took a huge amount of effort. Getting out of bed and facing the day was one of the hardest. The ongoing cycle of grief, depression, guilt, and anxiety just keeps rolling, and you can't see how this isn't going to be your life forever, but trust me, it won't be. It's crazy how the taboo that surrounds pregnancy loss, the stigma that is attached to miscarriage, stillbirth and neonatal death, or other people's discomfort, has made some people not want to talk about this time of sheer heartache when families should be celebrated for surviving and put on a pedestal. Losing a child is the worst pain imaginable; surviving it's nothing short of inspirational.

The part that I couldn't comprehend was that not many people ever asked to see photos of Noel and James, plus they completely dismissed the labour. It was a very different experience with my rainbow babies. Everyone wants to know the name you have chosen for your baby, how your labour was, and either see your baby or pictures of them, this is the polar opposite of giving birth to a baby born still. Yet it's still your child and the love you have for your babies whether they are here or not is beyond words. The day Noel and James were born was simply one of the best and worst days of our lives. It was the day we got to meet our two beautiful sons, our first born babies. We had dreamed of their faces for so long. Our hearts burst with love, yet it broke at the very same time, and our hopes and dreams were shattered.

There also appears to be a misconception that you can cheer someone up by skimming over a topic and finishing with a well-worn platitude such as, "everything happens for a reason" or "at least you know you can get pregnant". It makes you feel rubbish at a time when you already feel like your body has failed you and the guilt is overbearing. Just be there to listen and support your friend or family member. Never compare how they feel with benchmarks of others. People heal and grieve in their own time. Be there to ride the rollercoaster with them, through the ups and downs. As a friend or family member, don't be afraid to ask questions - it shows you care – and properly listen to the answers. Not asking can feel to the bereaved like you do not care; if you ask questions and that person cries, you haven't made them cry - the tears were already there waiting to fall. Crying is not a bad thing. Even now, after a stinker of a day, a good cry helps me, you sometimes need to give yourself permission to let it out.

In years gone by, it was expected that the bereaved would be in mourning for many months if not years, yet society now decrees that we simply brush ourselves down and get back to 'normal' or 'get over it' as soon as possible. Some processes in life just can't be rushed.

For me, it was about surviving each day and overcoming the first of everything.

These include (in no particular order)

- Leaving the house

- Seeing the neighbours

- Food shop (even though you might have no appetite)

- Phoning/visiting work

- Bumping into people who don't know about your loss

- Being on your own

- Returning to the hospital

- Birthdays/Christmas/Mother's Day and the first birthday

Surely I would be better after I had overcome the firsts of everything?

Perhaps if I started to keep myself a bit busier, so that I couldn't think (even though thinking and reliving everything kept me awake every night as I cried myself to sleep) – who has time to think when they are busy? Not me!

This was my survival guide; *keep busy and overcome the firsts.*

Most importantly I wanted to support my husband. His heart ached too, although dads or partners are often forgotten. Matt had been asked many times about how *I* was doing, but very few thought to ask how he was. I can only assume that those who only enquired after my wellbeing thought men simply have to be strong for their partners/wives. Erm, no, actually, they are surviving a total shit storm too.

Losing a baby doesn't just affect the person who was pregnant; the other parent feels the same heartache, helplessness, guilt, grief but they feel like they can't show it, it's not the 'done' thing, and that is sad. Support for the other parent can be a trip to the pub to get drunk and then throwing themselves straight back to work, as at this time dads and partners are only allowed two weeks paternity leave (and that's only if the baby is born after 24 weeks, before that they get nothing)! I can't even comprehend feeling that amount of grief and being expected to work two weeks later. It's totally bonkers! Although a new ruling on bereavement leave that is due out late 2018 is set to change all this - at last.

The ripple of grief, it doesn't just hit you, but your whole family – siblings, grandparents, nieces or nephews, the list goes on – friends, even work colleagues and midwives. This tragedy affects so many. We had no other children – Noel and James were the first grandchildren on both sides of the family. I can only imagine what it would be like if you had sunshine children (the term given to those born before loss) to care for and support too, but when I think about my parents, well, they not only felt their own grief for their grandchildren but also the pain and heartache they couldn't take away from me, their daughter.

Life continues even when you feel it shouldn't; the world somehow goes on turning, and other people's lives are still largely the same, even though for you the earth has spun off its axis and will forever be changed. That used to make me feel quite angry and bitter. And then you realise there are support networks available (that often you have had to search for and reach out to) and you meet lots of other families who have also lost a baby to share your heartache with. Then you are angry again as you realise the sheer amount of people affected by this. For so long, we felt alone and completely isolated – we didn't know anyone who had lost a baby – surely this hardly happened in the UK in 2011. Well it did, and it still does, it happens far too often. The loss of one baby is a year is too many. It's thought that one in four pregnancies end in miscarriage and currently, around 15 babies are stillborn or die during or soon after birth, every day in the UK.

Things that felt like an accomplishment in that first month …

- I brushed my hair

- I brushed my teeth

- I ate a meal that was nutritious

- . I stopped myself from getting drunk

- I got out of bed every day

- I smiled, maybe even laughed a little (but felt guilty as hell when I did)

Noel and James' funeral took place two weeks after their birth. I will never forget walking around Meadowhall Shopping Centre aimlessly. I had decided to go in a moment of thinking that I needed to do anything not to be at home, but when we were out, we couldn't wait to return home. I have no idea why we thought shopping would be a good idea. I'm sure we just wandered about without really looking at anything and praying that we didn't bump into anyone we knew who would ask where my bump had gone. Matt's phone rang, it was the funeral director asking what we wanted to have written on the plaque on their urn, and we were in Meadowhall, pretending to shop. I remember feeling so guilty for that, not guilt from anyone else, but the kind that you put on yourself.

The funeral was small and low key, held at a local crematorium. We were fortunate that the church in the next village to us had allowed us to have a headstone and bury our sons' ashes there as this is a place that meant a lot to us. It was where we had got married two years previously, I'd been christened, my parents had been married, and the list goes on. It's beautiful and peaceful. Because of this, the vicar came to perform the service, and it was really lovely from what I can remember. We were joined by close family, my best friend Ruth and three of the midwives from the hospital. I always remember my dad saying many years before that he had seen a baby coffin and it was the saddest thing he had ever seen. He wasn't wrong. I remember the funeral car arriving at the crematorium and walking over to look at the tiny coffin on the back seat that Noel and James were in together. I also remember having to leave and say goodbye again for the very last time. As we left, there were two squirrels outside playing together on the grass, right in front of where we were standing.

"White feathers fall, and squirrels appear, whenever Noel and James are near."

As we were waiting for Noel and James to be born Matt was adamant that we were going to book a holiday and go away. We booked a holiday for just after our six-week check at the hospital and went to Tenerife for a week. We felt we needed something else to focus on when in fact I think we just wanted to run away. We soon realised that running away doesn't change how you feel, and leaving the safety net of our humble abode was so much harder than we anticipated. Trying to sit around a pool or on the beach when you have just given birth to twins and your tummy shows it and feeling like everyone can tell, was difficult. How can you 'relax' when you are trying to switch your mind off from your emotions? It was like fighting a losing battle, and as much as the holiday was nice and we needed that time we were able to spend together it's something we never talk about now, it's like it didn't actually happen. Did we even go or did we dream it? Unfortunately one of the reasons I can remember this holiday now is that the first two rooms we were given in the hotel had cots in them. Oh, the irony.

Returning home after the holiday meant that Matt would be going back to work and it also meant that I would have to start thinking about my return to work. I can't say it was something I was looking forward to, but I felt it had to be done and part of me hoped that the 'normality' (there I go again!) and routine of returning to work would make me feel better. It had to happen at some point. Although the thought of going back to work filled me with dread, I was lucky enough to work with a small group of lovely ladies, all of whom had made a huge effort with us after the birth of Noel and James and I knew that they would help me again. Matt's work was fantastic too. I decided to go back to work in January – the New Year would mean a new start, and I had everything possible crossed that I would return to work pregnant.

Going back into work as a teacher when all your students saw you pregnant in September yet now you are returning to work without a bump and without any children at home was very hard for some of my students to comprehend. I don't blame them. I am not sure what or how I would have felt being a 16-year-old student faced with a tutor who had just lost her twin boys. Although the people I worked alongside were fantastic, that was not the case for my employers. My return to work was skimmed over (it was clear that they felt very uncomfortable) and on a later visit to my house, one person just stared at a picture of Noel and James that we had in OUR home. A picture of OUR children on display in OUR home was glared at, and it made me furious. I felt like they were being judged in what I had considered to be a safe environment – why not just ask to look?

Usually when you return to work from maternity, there is the option of a few stand-alone Keep In Touch days before you return, but other than that you just go back to work. If I'd returned from sick leave, my return would have been phased and probably very different to how it was. Apparently, I couldn't even have a 'proper' return to work as I wasn't breastfeeding (funny though, as late on I had one with Sebastian and he wasn't being breastfed) and therefore the day I went back to work it was like nothing had happened. Despite all this, I had the most precious little (probably lentil-sized) tinker hidden away in my tummy, and that was my whole focus. I would do anything, absolutely anything to avoid a single risk.

Yes, you read that right!

In the midst of this pain, we decided we had the strength to try just one more time for a baby. Before Noel and James were born, I had also experienced two early miscarriages, and the chances of actually being a parent to a living child felt impossible, but we had to give it one more shot. The twins were born at 26 weeks, and their due date was Christmas Eve. Even though we knew they would never reach that date, twins never do, it is a date that is easy to remember. That was the date that I also discovered I was pregnant again and here began our journey towards a rainbow baby.

As our first Christmas without the boys descended and the thought of returning to work afterwards became a reality, it was a time that felt very strange. Christmas is brilliant when you are happy and loving life, but when you're not, for whatever reason, it's proper crap. Constant reminders on TV about how happy, jolly and fun life should be and above all else spent with your family. Oh, the joys! When for us it was grim and a reminder of what we should have had – a crazy Christmas, with two new babies and not an ounce of sleep between us, yet instead nothing but sadness. We had been trying again, and I had been going to the gym, eating everything healthy, just in the hopes that it would all help me get pregnant again (what if I couldn't?) and make me feel like I had some control over my life once more. However, in all this, I was prepared to blow one day and drown my sorrows, because why shouldn't I? We were going to my mum and dad's, and I was going to be on it from the start until the end, trying not to think about how low and rubbish we would feel on Boxing Day. Now, we were trying, and I couldn't just drink all day if there was a tiny glimmer that I could actually be pregnant again (oh please, please, please!). So, on Noel and James' due date, Christmas Eve, I snuck off upstairs and did a sneaky test. I took myself off slyly for a few different reasons, and these were:

- I knew I'd get told off for being too eager (in a good way)

- I didn't want to get Matt's hopes up

- I didn't want to get my hopes up - I was only doing this to check, as I didn't think I actually was

- Self-denial that I was getting obsessed

A couple of moments passed, which felt like an eternity, but then there, right in front of me, was a cross. A CROSS!!!!!!! Chuffing hell, I was pregnant, and I hadn't anticipated it. I shouted Matt so loudly, and when he ran upstairs we both just stared at the test in disbelief, what were we going to do now? We felt ecstatic for about five seconds, and then the reality sank in thick and fast, what would happen if we lost this baby, would we survive? Would our relationship survive? Were we being selfish for trying again? Were we cruel being pregnant when we felt we would lose this baby too? Our minds were going into overdrive, and that wasn't going to calm down anytime soon – quite the opposite – it was going to get worse.

The survival guide still had the same ethos; keep busy and survive the firsts. Only one of the big 'firsts' was tomorrow and on top of everything we had a huge secret that was literally blowing our minds. Aargh!!!!!!!

Periods and early stages of pregnancy feel the same to me; I am sure there will be others who can tell, but to me, they feel exactly the same, and therefore your mind plays wonderful tricks on you to convince you otherwise. It's a time where you are completely obsessed about whether your boobs ache or not, whether your tummy aches for the right reasons and your hormones are at fever pitch. What a year 2011 had been; four pregnancies in a year; we were starting 2012 as we had started 2011 and that made me feel a bit nervous. Deep down, I am very superstitious, and even though I know how unlikely it is for lightning to strike in the same place twice it was very close timing to my first pregnancy, and that was another barrier to me not holding out much hope.

Hope is a funny word. When you feel like you have none, or you deny it from yourself. Secretly, in the deep, dark world of your mind, there's *always* a little hope. You either don't permit yourself to realise it, or you are totally afraid of the feeling. I was terrified of the feeling, and suppressing hope gave me what felt to me like some control of my emotions. If I just took things a day at a time and prepared myself for the worse and kept myself detached, then I would be safe, safe from all the heartache we could feel again. I knew this was a load of crap, but why listen to reason when you can convince and delude yourself to this new way of thinking... Sheer denial! Obviously, living with a mixture of obsession and denial was not going to get me far, but we will come to that a little later.

Ok, so just to recap....

So far, 2011 had thrown at us -

- Two miscarriages

- The loss of our beautiful boys Noel and

James at 26 weeks

- Planning a funeral

- Taking a last-minute desperation holiday

- Seeing Matt go back to work

- Dreading Christmas and the twins' due date

- Being pregnant again

What a year – one that you couldn't even make up if you tried – not that you would want to. Who could ever think of a year so completely and utterly devastating, with only the tiniest glimmer of hope and happiness appearing right at the end? With the knowledge that even that could be torn away from us in an instant too.

Could you imagine what I was like to live with? Hormone-tastic (poor Matt)!

There is one sure-fire way to keep yourself busier than you could ever imagine, so busy it could potentially distract you from your life, and that is fundraising. A common route for many people to follow after the loss of a baby, other family member or someone close to them. Somewhere there is a beacon of light in the darkest depths that can only be filled by doing something good and giving something back and that usually comes in the shape of raising funds for something.

This was the path that we decided to follow, after all, we had lots of thank yous to make for our care and support, and this would be a great way to show our appreciation. Also, our family and friends were keen to get stuck in and help us in some way, and this was a brilliant way to do it.

And while I can think, while I can talk
While I can stand, while I can walk
While I can dream, please let my dream
Come true

Walter Earl Brown- If I Can Dream (Elvis Presley)

Chapter 3

When it rains, look for rainbows

Okay, so you're pregnant again after a loss, surely that means you're 'fixed' and happy again?

Actually, how about, NO!

Now don't get me wrong, my rainbow babies have helped/saved me in so many ways but they will never replace the two children we have lost – nor would I ever want them to. Babies and children are not replaceable, and when I think how life should be, it should be crazy with four children very close in age.

The day I discovered I was pregnant again was another huge twist in our lives, another experience you can't explain unless you have walked this path yourself. But I'm going to try and give you an insight into all things rainbow.

There are a few terms used within the baby loss community to describe or explain a wide range of different terms. The ones commonly used are:

- Sunshine – a child born before a loss

- Angel – a baby who was miscarried or stillborn

- Rainbow – a child born after loss

Sunshine is bright, clear and uncomplicated – a beautiful ray of sunshine. An angel is self-explanatory, and even though I do use this term occasionally as it's just easy (there isn't an easily-recognised term used for a bereaved parent), it's not a term I would choose to use, and I can't explain why. Maybe it's because it sounds like they could do no wrong and that they are put on a pedestal, or that they are forever 'watching over us' – I hope wherever they are, they are having more fun than that. A lot of people use the terms angel baby, angel mummy, angel daddy and I do think it's nice, it's just not for me. Rainbow; a rainbow shows that a family has been through a storm, in fact, the storm is still there, and the sky can still be dark and the stormy times will never be forgotten. However, there is light, colour, hope in a rainbow. You might have heard the lovely short poem,

Everyone wants happiness; nobody wants pain,

But you can't have a rainbow, without a little rain.

Well, this is true! Again, not everyone is a fan of these terms, but for me, I do relate to the affection behind the term rainbow baby. And here is where my rainbow obsession begins – not bad for someone whose favourite colour and wardrobe contents contain black, black and more black!

You look to the sky and see a rainbow, and it makes you smile; they are glorious. You can't touch one though, and the closer you get, the further away the rainbow seems to be, a bit like a rainbow pregnancy and the daily chasing of rainbows.

When you are trying to conceive, you desperately want to be pregnant – everyone does – and that is natural. When you are trying again after loss, I felt that I was desperate to be pregnant again, but I was also completely terrified.

* * * *

Let me take you back; I was 29 years old, in good health and growing two beautiful boys in my womb, yet they died, and I had had no idea. I had been at home, washing baby clothes (never did that whilst pregnant again!), tidying the house, blissfully unaware that in a couple of hours my life would change forever as we discovered our boys had passed away. How could I not know that? What sort of mum was I? Why had my body failed us so badly? Surely there is a mother's intuition? Everyone always tells you this. I felt that I should have known and mentally this destroys you for a long time, in fact, I don't think that 'guilt' ever goes away.

A life surrounded by 'what ifs'.

- What if I'd had a scan that day?

- What if I'd seen my midwife?

- What if I'd not been so busy and could

remember when I had last felt them move?

- What if I'd missed the warning signs?

- What if I'd gone to the hospital sooner?

- What if, what if, what if …

Mental torture!

Like most parents, I had done nothing wrong and had tried my best. I read every pregnancy book going and followed the rules to the letter (first time for everything) but it happened in my body, and therefore I felt like it was my fault and my body had failed me on a monumental scale. I hated myself, and I am sure if I looked in a dictionary right now, the word guilt would feature under mother, mum, and mummy. It sits together hand in hand, and I feel it constantly with my rainbows. Mums are far too hard on themselves, but it's because they want to be the best they can be and give the best life possible for their children.

You can't always win though, don't forget we have to be back in our jeans within six weeks, or you've let yourself go, but don't get too thin; stay at home to nurture your offspring or return to full-time work to set a good example… the list is endless. I am of the opinion that you should do what suits you and your family and be true to yourself. There will always be too many people judging parenting skills, who knows why. Don't even get me started on the term 'hands-on Dad' or "who is babysitting, Dad?" It's just being a parent. If you are a mum reading this, you are bloody ace and doing a brilliant job, don't ever forget that!! Dads and partners: you're pretty amazing too (never forget the other half of the parenting team)!

Okay, so we've covered guilt. This is only one of the emotions you will feel on a daily basis to the most extreme of levels during a rainbow pregnancy and you have to roll with it; you have no choice. I was pregnant for the fourth time this year and I had been 26 weeks pregnant with twins only three months before this date. This really takes its toll on your body physically never mind your mental health. I felt like I had been pregnant for about five years already, and each day of a rainbow pregnancy feels like an eternity; yet now I look back and I think it went in the blink of an eye.

So there we were, pregnant again with our longed for rainbow. Who were we going to tell and when? How did we actually feel? I can't even recall all of the details! I think we were just in total shock in those first few days and weeks.

If I remember correctly, I think we kept it to ourselves until after Christmas Day. It is hard telling your family and friends again even though you know everyone is rooting for you and that they are desperate to hear your good news. But as soon as the words leave your lips, it seems to become more of a reality, and we kept it to ourselves for as long as we could so that we could process the news ourselves. Now, I am good – amazing in fact – at keeping secrets for others, but cannot help but blurt out anything about me – I am the worst liar in the world and if anyone asked me anything about the prospect of another pregnancy or even how I was doing I was sure it would be written all over my face. As soon as possible we called our midwife, who luckily booked us in for an early scan at about seven weeks, so only three weeks to wait! Only three weeks. Crikey, that still seemed forever away at that point, and I had no idea how we would cope.

Somehow we did get through those initial weeks, and our scan day finally came. We saw a beautiful little beating rainbow heart. I wished I could just fall asleep and wake up at 36 weeks ready to give birth because the thought of waiting that long was unbearable. It would be awful if you did though and missed seeing your beautiful bump grow, feeling all of the kicks and hiccups your baby gives you. Usually, when you are wired up to a monitoring machine because you have convinced yourself you haven't felt baby move all day, and now you are hysterical, in hospital, being monitored in the middle of the night in the midst of a panic attack* and looking daft as you have the wriggliest baby ever! We should have known he was going to be a little rascal.

*The amount of times I dragged Matt out of bed in the middle of the night because of panic attacks, lack of movements, pure fear/anxiety resulting in us heading up to the hospital felt endless.

Our midwife was fantastic. She saw me regularly and allowed me to drop in for reassurance sessions, where she would listen in to baby's heartbeat when I was low and struggling. I know that listening to a heartbeat doesn't necessarily mean anything. It doesn't always highlight if anything is wrong with baby, but for that few moments of listening to bumpity bumps of a tiny but very strong heartbeat is sheer bliss and then as soon as you leave the clinic you can feel as scared as when you walked in. It's like an addiction that can never be satisfied. Every bit of light relief you feel in a rainbow pregnancy is very short-lived, plus any build up to appointments and scans ties your stomach into knots and turns you into an insomniac. I can remember the feeling of being sat in the sonography waiting room now, with my legs shaking so badly I felt like I would have to be carried in and a thousand nervous trips to the toilet when you're trying to keep a full bladder for a better view of your precious baby. You just wait, wait for the next appointment, wait for a new day, wait for a new week, wait to reach 12 weeks, wait to reach 24 weeks, wait for everything. What is the best way to pass the time? Oh yes, keep busy.

Back to my top survival guide! Keep busy and survive

the firsts of everything.

On top of surviving the firsts of everything in our journey of grief, we were also surviving them whilst pregnant again – so there was a whole load more firsts and a bucket-load of hormones in the mix of it all. Alongside this, you search for and meet so many other bereaved families to give you hope and make you feel less isolated. But they have their stories too, and it can start to make you worry about all the possible ways in which babies can die, as their experiences are often very different to your own. And don't even get me started on the internet as that will literally blow your mind.he hea

It also makes you talk to complete strangers about the most personal things you have been feeling, both physically and mentally, in great detail. This is why the internet and social media can be so good. These are things you would probably never think of discussing normally, but this is not a normal situation – you become so obsessed and focussed on your babies (those that have died as well as your new little rainbow) that they are all you can think about. I wouldn't be half the person I am now without these wonderful people who support you, and I am going to tell you lots more about how wonderful they are very soon.

Now I won't write here some of the things you search for, as you don't need to know (plus it might put you off your tea) but you search for everything, desperately wanting to find someone who has experienced exactly the same as you and it has all turned out alright. Unfortunately, when you look on the internet you may as well resign yourself to the fact that it's going to be bad and full of negativity because let's face it, more people write or tell you about bad things that have happened rather than good, but does that stop you looking? No.

Days turned into weeks and weeks into months. I was back at work with my lovely colleagues, battling through each day, and struggling to be motivated about anything. I felt drained by grief as well as growing a new little person, and all my strength and determination was put into survival. My enthusiasm for my job went down the pan. Working in beauty therapy means the use of lots of chemicals and essential oils, all of which terrified me now. There was no way my new baby was going to be put in any jeopardy, and I excluded myself from anything that didn't quite sit right, even though deep down I knew I would probably be okay. But I didn't care; this was the first time in my life I was going to be selfish, and I felt like I had just reason.

Being back at work was so much harder than I anticipated and when you are back, you're back in the full throttle of things – there are no allowances made, and part of you understands – why should there be really? Pregnancy isn't an illness; it's a very normal part of life for millions of women around the world, many of whom continue working throughout much of their pregnancies without any issues. If you are back at work, you should be able to do your job, but you don't actually know that until you start back, and when you do, you are trapped. My poor colleagues had to put up with A LOT of crying and, eventually, when I was 24 weeks pregnant, I went off sick for a few days due to the fear of approaching the dreaded 26-week mark. I never went back. I was just too terrified. The 40-minute drive to work scared me in case I had to brake too hard, and the seatbelt was tight on my tummy; I wanted to be close to home in case my waters broke unexpectedly again. I just wanted to be a hermit until the end of my pregnancy.

Being off work sounds like a great idea, but going back to the great achievements of getting out of bed and brushing your hair again soon come back. I was pregnant and shattered, emotional and drained, and there was nothing at all at home to distract me. There was no way on earth that I would sort out any baby things, as that is what I had been doing when my waters had broken, surely that was a jinx? Anyway, how could I sort them out when I didn't even know if I would have a baby to bring home?

The black cloud of dread...

Being pregnant after a loss is like walking around with a cloud of impending doom over your head. I know I am making this sound so negative, but it's true. Things can happen and change so quickly, and you spend your life pre-empting something that 'could' happen, not allowing yourself to imagine the future and what it holds and only living in that particular moment. It stops you from living life;

your mind consumes you with negative and fearful thoughts that talk to you morning and night. So I resorted back to my old faithful bookworm lifestyle and visited the library every couple of days, taking out as many trashy novels or horrors that I could read and filled my life with fantasy. In between this I knitted (badly) and planned our fundraising efforts. Anything to occupy my mind in the safe four walls of our house and that would stop me thinking. But in reality, nothing can stop that from happening, and the plan to keep the thoughts at bay in the daytime meant they became even worse at night. I lost count of the amount of times we travelled up to the hospital in the middle of the night because I was having a panic attack, due to convincing myself something was wrong or I hadn't felt baby move. We live in a small town, and our local hospital had only five birth rooms, so in comparison to others, it is small. This was an advantage as we got to know so many of the staff either through our pregnancies, the birth of Noel and James or through our rainbow pregnancy.

The three midwives who were there at the birth of the twins, plus the midwives that looked after us post birth were unbelievable. They were incredible! They are magnificent! In a non-weird way, I think I actually love them – as crazy as this sounds. Being with someone so intensely through the most horrific time of your life can go one of two ways, and for us, we were blessed it went the best way it could. The care was faultless; the compassion they showed, and the fact that they went above and beyond their role to give us the best care and support we could receive meant the world to us. We weren't judged, we weren't forced to make any decisions that we weren't ready to make, and my whole family was treated with the utmost respect. Writing this now, I have tears in my eyes and these three ladies, in particular, will have a special place in our hearts forever.

Of course, when you have had such a wonderful experience in tragic circumstances, you wish you could just have the same team deliver your rainbow. Unfortunately, this didn't happen, but our experiences were still good.

Pregnancy after loss doesn't just affect you; it affects everyone who is close to you. Wanting to know everything because they care about and love you but sometimes it's hard to share and let people in because you're afraid of them being hurt again too. Matt would ask me constantly if I felt OK, his hands always feeling for reassuring kicks and his eyes constantly checking that I wasn't lying when I said I was fine; what a rock.

Unfortunately, not all couples survive after their baby dies, the pressure of the different ways in which people grieve can tear them apart. Some people want to talk and can't understand why their partners don't. There are many different scenarios, and I'm not surprised it happens. It's pretty much the shittiest thing that can happen to anyone and changes your perspectives and lives forever. For us, it made us stronger than we had ever been, even though I tried so hard not to look at Matt and feel how much I thought I had let him down, even though he would absolutely object to such a thing.

We discovered our rainbow baby was a boy at 16 weeks and decided on the name Sebastian Joel. Sebastian was a name contender for the twins, but we had decided to go for Noel (due Christmas Eve and because of my secret love for Noel Fielding), plus

James at it's Matt's middle name. We loved the name Sebastian, and little Sebbyroo (with his anterior placenta, tinker!) looked super cute on each scan photo. He melted our hearts. Joel was a combination of Noel and James, his big brothers watching over him and (hopefully) helping him arrive safely.

The build-up to the 26-week mark was awful. I was off work, and I just felt like I couldn't cope any longer and wanted to cocoon myself in my home environment, determined I would go back afterwards as if the fear would disappear after the 26-week mark, but of course, it didn't. I was now in unknown territory and more terrified than ever. I hadn't been this pregnant before, and I didn't know how I should be feeling or anything. I just wanted a date for induction, and my dreams as I slept were becoming more terrifying by the night. The main dream (nightmare) I had was telling people I was pregnant and them looking at me, and I had no bump. I would be trying to convince them and even screaming at them to say that I was pregnant, but no one believed me – or watching other people giving birth for me as I obviously felt incapable of doing it myself. I wanted a date for induction, but what if that day was a day too late? What if my baby died the day before induction and it was my fault for not pushing for it sooner? The guilt and fear were escalating to an enormous scale and was not slowing down. My mind thought about every situation as I tried to mentally prepare myself for it. What I didn't prepare myself for, was being a parent – that was something I didn't even dare to think about.

After lots of scans, trips to the hospital, midwives appointment and tears it was finally agreed by the hospital that I would start having sweeps from 36 weeks and could begin the induction process at 37 weeks. After 36 weeks of desperately trying to keep a baby in, I never realised how difficult it would be to get one out when they are nice and comfy still in your womb. Naively, I thought one sweep would do the trick.... Oh, how I laugh typing this! A couple of sweeps and not even a Braxton hick meant that induction was booked at 37 weeks and I couldn't wait to take residence in the hospital on one of those incredible monitoring machines, knowing that I was in safe hands. It was August, the London Olympics had just finished, and it was hot! Especially hot on an observation bay, with no windows, and sat in the same space I was told the worst news imaginable with Noel and James.

Induction started, but nothing happened. We kept being told it was going to be a long process, but I didn't listen. My waters had broken naturally with the twins, and they were born the next day, so surely it would be that easy again?

Walking miles, bouncing on a ball and generally losing the will to live summed up the 14th August! I just want my baby!!!!!! Why can't someone just get him out!!!!

I was exhausted; not sleeping for days beforehand and the worry of the day had left me shattered and eventually we were given a birth room at 8pm that night. Now surely that is a good sign? Actually in the room where we would give birth now, and there was no way I was going to leave it without our baby.

During the night my waters were broken, and the contractions came, but not regularly enough, and I had to be hooked up to the dreaded drip to get them kick-started again. Crikey that stuff is vicious!

It works like a dream, but it was very hard going. I had morphine for the pain, but it made me ill, so eventually, I agreed to have an epidural. Leaning forward and sitting still when you have approx. 10 seconds between each contraction in order to have a huge needle inserted into your spine is scary, and the first one didn't work, so it had to be done again. I will always remember the anaesthetist saying, "this will be the last contraction you will feel" and laying back on the bed thinking, "Well, thank fuck for that!" before the contractions kicked straight back in again and I was screaming, thinking what the hell has happened! The anaesthetist asked when I was last examined, by which point the midwife could see Sebastian's head, and I started to push. Three wonderful midwives encouraging me and supporting me to push, I felt like giving in. I hadn't thought this far, and now I was scared – something could still happen; I was so out of control, and I was terrified.

One final push and our beautiful rainbow son was placed on my chest. He was alive... ALIVE!!!!!!

ALIVE!!!

His bottom lip was quivering with the screaming, and I just froze.

Oh. My. God

Fu-cking-hell.

I actually think I was in shock; he took our breath away, but I felt like I just stared and was still for so long because I couldn't believe Sebastian was here: alive, screaming, in our arms and we could take him home to keep. Emotionally and physically I was well and truly exhausted, but he was in our arms now, and there was no way on earth I was going to let go. We couldn't take our eyes off him, and I felt invincible like I could achieve absolutely anything. After all, Sebastian had felt like an impossibility, and now he was here – I could do anything. In fact, if my legs had been working properly after the epidural and I had not felt like my insides were going to drop out, I would have done a lap of honour around the hospital. Looking at our beautiful boy now, he still makes me feel that way. Sebastian makes me feel so proud, even though at times I felt that we had no hope – he kept going, and now he was here, in our arms and bloody gorgeous.

I can't even explain it.

Sheer bliss! (And guilt, lots more guilt) Accompanied by absolute elation!

We felt happy, and our family and friends were overjoyed for us, but does that mean we had forgotten or were going to forget our two beautiful boys who came before him? No, absolutely not, but those first few months left me wracked with more guilt. How can I wish for them to be here as that would mean I wouldn't have Sebastian and vice versa. It took a long time to turn that voice off in my head. Sebastian never replaced his brothers, and so he shouldn't, but he helped us heal in so many ways, and now we were his parents, something we didn't dare to dream about. We hadn't got a single thing out for him at home (just in case). We were on cloud nine; the happiest I had felt in forever and ready to take on the world.

And here is where our rainbow parenting journey begins.

Little darling, I believe you could

Help me a lot

Just take my hand

And lead me where you will

Joan Anita Barbara Armatrading- Love and Affection

Chapter 4

Parenting after loss- a.k.a. WTF!

So there I was, with a brand new baby in my arms and not just any baby – our very special rainbow baby. He was cuddled, kissed and adored every second by our close family and us. We were then moved to the maternity ward to get some 'rest'. If you've ever tried to sleep on a maternity ward, you will know that rest is pretty impossible. Not only do you have your bundle of joy to stare at (he really was ours to keep!) but the buzz you have after birth is unreal. It leaves you physically exhausted, but I just couldn't sleep. Every murmur of a baby on the ward made me sit up to check Sebastian was okay or if he needed feeding, etc. In all honesty, I wanted to hold him and never let him go, plus I think I was still in shock and felt like my life was a dream, and at any moment I would wake up, still pregnant and frightened.

I was deluded to think that the worry would be easier after the birth of our beautiful rainbow; I used to think that when I could actually look at Sebastian, it would make me feel easier and less afraid as I would be able to see what was wrong with him. But I had never looked after a newborn baby before, and every sound, movement lack of or too much sleep, lack of or too much food made me feel (like most new mums no doubt) anxious. You just want to do the right thing and – going back to the feelings of guilt – in a way I do think that feeling makes us good mums as it means we are trying so hard to do our best, but the levels of guilt need to be manageable.

I tested positive for Group B Strep after the birth of Noel and James and therefore opted for antibiotics in my labour with Sebastian, to reduce the risk of infection for him and for me. Because of this, we were in hospital slightly longer as they monitored Sebastian at regular intervals to make sure he was okay.

When we left the hospital to make our journey home in the car, it all felt so very different from the last time we had left after giving birth. I was sat in the back with our baby boy, feeling like we had our whole lives ahead of us, instead of the feeling of wanting to go to bed and never wake up again.

At home, there wasn't a single thing out and ready – what a total nightmare! We hadn't wanted to jinx anything, which sounds totally bonkers now, but we didn't want to take any risks by getting our hopes up and taking things out to prepare ourselves for a new baby if it all ended in tragedy again. At home, the steriliser was still in a box, the Moses basket was still wrapped up, and everything was packed away.

The first few weeks of Sebastian's life were filled with so many visitors. Our friends and family couldn't wait to meet him, and we couldn't blame them – who wouldn't want a cuddle and a squeeze with our beautiful rainbow! It is hard though, as a mum who has just given birth and is still struggling with anxiety, to hand your precious baby over to others for a large proportion of the day. As much as you want to share the love and are incredibly grateful for the support and care everyone is giving you, part of you just wants your baby for yourself, just like it has been for the last nine months.

After Matt returned to work and most of our visitors dried up, the reality of being a parent on my own during the daytime sank in, and my Health Visitor recommended going to some playgroups. Bearing in mind, I only saw my Health Visitor once, despite our history of loss and being within the first year of grief! I just had a feeling that playgroups would not be my cup of tea before I even went; the first session I ever went to was at 9am, yes 9am! Surely anyone that has had children knows how impossible it can be to leave the house before at least 11am! I set my alarm for 5am to get everything ready – it was on the levels of military precision, and I was still late getting there (story of my life). I can't remember exactly how long I was there for before someone asked if Sebastian was my first child, and I said no actually he has two older twin brothers, but they were stillborn. It was a day I felt strong enough to say it and 'get it out of the way' so to speak, I just wanted people to know, so they never asked me again. Unfortunately, the reaction I received was uncomfortable; I don't want someone's sympathy, I am just answering truthfully, and this really put me off for a long time. I forced myself to go a few more times as it seemed the 'done' thing, but they weren't for me, nor were baby weigh-ins, and I think a large part of that was the small talk that is involved with meeting other people for the first time when you have children with you. For me, it has too often become awkward and only increased my sense of isolation and frustration that society still has so long to go before bereaved parents feel able to talk about all of their children freely.

I did take Sebastian a few times to be weighed. It seemed to be what everyone else did, and lots of mums talk about weight, so it adds to the conversation. However, I only really went because something was not quite right with Sebastian and his feeding and I couldn't work it out – was I being neurotic? Are all babies like this? We were bottle feeding – were we doing it right?

I struggled with breastfeeding – I am not sure why – probably due to confidence, or the fact that the smell of my milk turned my stomach. The last time my milk came it was a cruel reminder that even though my body had failed me and Noel and James, it never failed in bringing my milk (apparently you can take a tablet to stop this, but I didn't know at the time). It's such a shame I felt like that, but I'm sure it was some form of Post Traumatic Stress Disorder (PTSD). No one is ever there to support you with bottle feeding, yet it can seem so scary for any parent doing it for the first time, let alone a mum struggling with anxiety.

Here are a few of the million questions we had:

- Why have a six-bottle steriliser to only sterilise one bottle at a time

- Do you have to dry a sterilised bottle?

- How much is too much milk?

- Too little?

- Do I really have to sterilise a bottle, boil the kettle and wait for it to cool for 30 minutes at 2am with a screaming baby?

- How do you actually wind a baby?

Surely there are ways people survive night feeds without going insane or considering divorce! Thank goodness for the bottle makers that came out too late for Sebastian but just in time for our second rainbow.

We bought pre-prepared milk to warm up to save the drama in the night, but Sebastian was still struggling with his feeds and was super windy. After numerous trips to the baby clinic, doctors and so on, finally Sebastian was confirmed as lactose intolerant, and the first bottle of lactose-free milk was a game changer. It went down like a treat, stayed down and he wasn't crying, result!

Maybe I did have a mother's intuition after all (or is it still a token phrase?).

A month and a day after Sebastian's birth was Noel and James' first birthday. The build-up was horrific; my hormones were already everywhere, and life was bittersweet with a beautiful new rainbow, topped with record levels of anxiety and zero sleep. We decided to have a small tea party with our close family and a balloon release. The day was peaceful, as I discovered was the case with all anniversaries and birthdays. The build-up does take its toll on you as you relive each day in your mind and think of all the *what ifs*, but the day itself is usually peaceful and calm. This meant we had 'survived' all the firsts. Hurrah! Did we feel any better? No. Now all the firsts had passed, and our rainbow was safe and sound in our arms, what did we have to focus on now? Then I remembered the overwhelming urge to keep myself busy was still at large, and we still had plans to fundraise, so the combination of both fundraising and a newborn kept me thinking and busy all day long.

One thing to get yourself in a fluster about is the word ROUTINE! It does make me chuckle now, but at the time it was nearly a full-on obsession, and what for? I'm not one for routine and forced rules, but everyone seems to do it, so it's normal right? To some extent, yes, you need routine, as you would never leave the house, nor would your children ever go to bed. You definitely need this with boundaries too when your child gets older, but there is absolutely nothing wrong with cuddling your baby whilst they are sleeping. I'd give my right arm to do that now.

Daytime naps are a distant memory in our house, but when they did exist, it felt like a time to do a weeks' worth of jobs in about 20 minutes. A bomb could have gone off, and Sebastian would have stayed asleep, but the notion of me drinking a hot coffee or eating a meal made his eyes fly open in seconds! I wish I hadn't felt the urge to fill time and just spent time for me – watching the TV or enjoying a bath (crikey!) or just sitting down reading a book whilst our gorgeous little boy lay asleep next to me. Oh, I soon lost count of how many times I did watch his tiny chest rise and fall though, just to make sure he was still okay. Thank goodness for the sensory mat baby monitors, or I think I would have lost all sanity. For those that haven't used these monitors, this is how they work: the baby monitor works like any others, and you can hear your baby cooing or crying via it. It's also attached to a mat approximately the size of a table mat which fits underneath the cot mattress and monitors a baby's movement, in particular, their breathing. If the baby stops breathing/moving an alarm sounds and you rush in to check your baby.

Every time this alarm goes off, you crap yourself! Slightly frightened at what you may face when you burst into the nursery, which in reality is usually when they have wriggled slightly from the mat. Phew! When the monitor was turned on, it made a slight ticking sound which put our minds at ease if we woke in the night – just to hear the continuous sound was an amazing source of reassurance and thank goodness we had access to this.

Anxiety is a right shitter. If you are feeling anxious, you are worried about the future; if you are depressed, you are generally worried about the past. Being anxious makes sense in a rainbow pregnancy, but surely it should find itself an off switch and take a hike after the birth? Unfortunately, it doesn't work this way, even though I thought that it would. There's no magical switch that turns off your anxiety after the event you were worried about as there are now loads of other things to think and fret about. Feelings of worry about being a parent, about what the future holds, and the expectations you have of yourself and others have around you – even if they aren't on a grand scale – they soon mount up. After

Sebastian was born, I thought my anxiety would fade, and even though I knew I would still be grieving and carrying around a feeling of guilt, I thought I would be able to manage this is in a different way. How wrong could I be? When you are in the mindset of worry and dread, you can't just switch your mind off, no matter how hard you try. Instead, you find ways to help yourself overcome this, or embrace the new you. After all, you will never be the person you once were, and why would you ever want to be.

I think it took me six months to realise Sebastian was here to stay and to be released from part of the fog. Those first six months are a bit hazy, and I do feel that has to do with trying to avoid certain social situations in fear of other's reactions or questions.

All of the difficulties aside, being Sebastian's mum is one of the best things in the world, and he brings so much joy to our world.

One of the things that forced me out of the house on a weekly visit was a lovely trip to Rufford Abbey with a couple of my friends from work who were either part-time or also on maternity leave. A stroll around the lake, a coffee, and a good old natter were just what we needed. They had been amongst the friends who had been there for the worst time of my life and therefore deserved to also be there for the good times. Their support and words of wisdom helped me tremendously – I felt like Emma again and less isolated.

During our weekly visits, my friend Lisa and I used to discuss fundraising. We talked about getting more involved and giving more back and eventually decided to set up 'JOEL The Complete Package'. The name came from the combination of Noel and James' names and Sebastian's middle name; 'The Complete Package' meant that we would fundraise and give back to those who offered support to us, as well as signpost to others where needed. JOEL would be the name used to fundraise for our local Sands group and Bassetlaw Hospital through a range of Family Fun Days and enable us to bring the community together. We planned our first event in Mansfield for the November after Sebastian was born. It certainly worked to keep us busy, and I absolutely loved the networking. It was a fantastic way to talk about my family without awkwardness and it was so liberating and empowering. Our first event was a huge success, and we soon planned our next three events over the course of six months in Worksop and Mansfield. We met some wonderful small businesses, and fantastic people, who jumped on board with the ethos of JOEL and I couldn't believe the stories I heard at the events from others who had their own story to tell – some from many years ago.

So, we were not the only ones to feel alone through pregnancy and parenting after loss, and there was nothing else filling that gap. Maybe this was where JOEL could step in.

I knew there were others that felt the same way as I did; I had met families at other groups and events. We knew there was nothing else available because we had searched high and low for it. This was our chance, and the chance for many other families to go to playgroups with their sunshine or rainbow children and seek support without feeling uncomfortable and fearful of being asked awkward questions. Perhaps our rainbows could grow up knowing that they were not alone in the loss of a sibling? Perhaps a family

COULD be celebrated as a whole? And this was the start of JOEL as we know it today.

After a year of maternity leave, and with total dread, I returned to work. We had moved premises, and it felt like I had returned to a new job. I still didn't feel supported, and the feeling grew that perhaps this was not what I wanted any more – so I took voluntary redundancy and spent a few years not knowing what I should be doing. Trying to find part-time work that still allows precious family time at weekends and evenings is difficult. I simply didn't know what I wanted anymore, I was a different person. Anyway, we had given everything to have Sebastian, so why would I want to work full-time and miss everything; it was tough enough for Matt to have to do that.

So, surely this was the time to have another baby?

We knew we wanted to try again; we talked about it as soon as Sebastian was born. We didn't want Sebastian to grow up without living siblings (not that there is anything wrong with that necessarily) but we knew that if we waited too long after he was born, we probably wouldn't have had the guts to go for it. We were also conscious of the thought that if we lost another baby, Sebastian would be too young to understand (sounds ridiculous now). We went on a wonderful family holiday to Italy with my parents and brother a couple of days after Sebastian's first birthday and a week after we returned I discovered I was pregnant again!

We don't do anything by halves...

Sebastian was now one year old and like a rocket. He was (still is) into everything and a total rascal; Noel and James' second birthday was fast approaching, and now I was pregnant again. What a rollercoaster! We had done it before, and we could do it again, only this time we had a one-year-old tinker, and we had made a pretty good job of bringing him up so far, so we felt that this pregnancy was a little bit achievable. The glimmer of a tiny bit more hope this time around was amazing as well as slightly worrying, but we also had someone to keep us busy and take our minds off the time and how quickly, or not, it was passing.

Being a parent is the hardest and most rewarding job in the world – watching your children's character develop, finding out what they love – plus lots of cuddles and laughter are simply the best. It was always in the back of my mind as to how I might have parented before losing babies, but this is something I would never know. Plus I wrestled with the challenge of how to tell Sebastian about his older brothers; they too play a huge part in our lives, and we love our children equally. From the day Sebastian was born, he was told all about his big brothers as was their younger sister Polly. We have always been open and honest when Sebastian and Polly have asked questions about their older brothers, avoiding terms such as "fell asleep" or "too poorly".

Even in the summer

Even in the spring

You can never get too much of

A wonderful thing

PJ Harvey- This is Love

Chapter 5

Pot of gold

Being pregnant with my second rainbow baby brought back so many emotions, ones that I had hidden far away in the depths of my mind.

There was one big factor that helped this time, and that was Sebastian. I knew having a living baby was an actual possibility now; I had done it once before, so surely I could do it again? On top of this, Sebastian was a huge distraction, and I was about to start a new job, so everything felt good.

We had been fundraising for JOEL for the last year, and the focus of everything together made me feel more pre-occupied and have a tiny, tiny element of confidence, although I would never have dared to admit it at the time.

The one thing that worried me now was the lack of care and support. If I revealed the tinges of hope I was experiencing more of this time, then health professionals would see absolutely no reason to give me the extra scans and appointments I had benefited from previously. What would I do if this happened? It would be a total nightmare.

As always, I experienced bleeding in the early stages so I had an early scan which offered some reassurance. Sebastian stopped my days from feeling like an eternity and we kept going; every night I went to bed thinking, "I am still pregnant, and today has been good". I felt great this time, I didn't feel sick, just tired, and that was no wonder as Sebastian used to wake at 4.30am pretty much every day (I don't miss that). Any non-pregnant person would be knackered, never mind when you're growing a precious little life inside your tummy. We binge-watched Breaking Bad every evening until I fell asleep and that's how we kept going. I was scanned at 12 weeks, and my next scan would be at 20 weeks, the longest time I had ever gone. Scans can be traumatic, and even though they offer some reassurance and you get to see your beautiful baby, the days and nights before the next scan are often filled with worry and panic – feeling sick to your stomach. The waiting room still makes me anxious when I see it now. I was adamant that I would be okay, but as the 16-week mark approached, I started to feel nervous and wanted the reassurance of another scan.

I paid for a private scan, and I booked it as a surprise for Matt's birthday, only to be filled with dread. What if we were told bad news for his birthday? Silly really, as bad news and heartache wouldn't make any difference to what the day is.

We went for the scan with Sebastian. It was a lovely peaceful room, and as soon as the ultrasound was placed on my tummy it was plain to see that our little tinker was a girl! A GIRL! We were so happy!

Baby Petulla grew big and strong, and she was very kind with her regular kicks. It was a fabulous pregnancy and looking back I did enjoy it as much as was possible. I tried my hardest anyway as I knew this would be the last time I would be pregnant. EVER! It's very hard to make the middle of the night trips to the labour ward with a one-year-old though, so anxiety on a night time was bad.

Mentally, that was it for us. We couldn't handle more worry, anxiety and fear. We just wanted to start living again and enjoying making the most of what we had. Near the end of our pregnancy, we agreed that would be it, all being well, and after a year Matt would make a trip to the hospital to make sure we would never be surprised. It felt weird drawing a line under this part of our lives, but it also felt like a weight had been lifted.

Petulla was due in May, a funny old month in our family as it seems to be the month filled with anniversaries of other family members no longer with us. We felt it would be good to have something positive to celebrate in May, although potentially our baby could have been born in April if I was induced at 37 weeks as with Sebastian.

Surprisingly, I was only classed as high risk because of my Rheumatoid Arthritis, and medication, so I was scanned after 30 weeks. They told me I wouldn't go past 40 weeks, but they wanted to start my induction at 40 weeks exactly. I wasn't happy. Eventually, after much bartering, it was agreed that I would be induced at 39 weeks and I would be booked in on the 1st May. During this time, my grandma, who had had poor health for years, bless her, was starting to get worse. She was one of the few people we told our name choices to, and we tried to make the most of spending time with her. She was so excited to become a great grandma again and to a girl this time. By the time the 1st of May came, my grandma was very poorly, and we knew time was precious. My poor mum not only had to care and make the most of time left with her but also had to think about her daughter being ready to have another baby at any day; a daughter who was terrified. It must have been totally mind-blowing. Now I have my own daughter; I can't imagine being in that position.

On the 1st of May, I took my hospital bag and Matt and I went to the labour ward to start my induction. We waited and waited and waited. The labour ward was busy, and soon it was dinner time; I knew deep down that they wouldn't do anything to induce me on that day, but I didn't want to go home and was determined I wouldn't leave without our rainbow. At 5pm, feeling dreadful, I was sent home, feeling gutted. We picked up Sebastian and went to visit my grandma with all my family (we only have a small family really) as she was at home. My grandma was laid on a bed in the front room, and we all sat there chatting about times we had together. Most of those conversations involved my Uncle Paul who had been taken far too soon years before, as this day would have been his birthday. He was a gentle giant, hilarious, and an all-round legend. It was a lovely time sat there altogether, and I am so grateful I was sent home as I would have missed out on so much.

The next morning, we awoke early as we were heading to the hospital for our induction and the phone rang. I knew who it would be; it was my mum. My grandma had passed away a couple of hours before. We went to the hospital with an ache in our hearts, knowing she was finally at peace, but never having had the chance to meet our baby girl. We decided that if our baby was born that day, she would have an extra middle name, my grandma's middle name, Ann.

The hospital was amazing, and I was overjoyed that

our midwife was one of the incredible midwives who had delivered Noel and James. I knew we were in great hands and this was it. My waters were broken within ten minutes of being there, and I felt very overwhelmed. It was all happening so fast and much quicker than we had anticipated. When my contractions didn't progress, I opted for an epidural as soon as the dreaded drip was mentioned (it really is evil) and laid on my left-hand side (because baby's heart rate dropped if I laid any other way). I could feel tightening, but otherwise, I felt great. Previously I had had morphine in both labours and felt completely off my face and out of control, this time I just had an epidural so the pain was reduced, but I was fully aware of what was happening. At 5.30pm I knew I needed to push, but they thought I wasn't quite ready; I had been dilating slowly, but there I was, ready to go and after only a few pushes our beautiful baby girl Polly Jane Ann was welcomed into the world – with lots of screams – and I was on the verge of hysterics. What a day! Knowing our family was now completed was relief beyond words; Polly was our final addition, and she was absolutely perfect. She was weighed and a hat placed on her head, which just so happened to be one of the hats my mum had knitted and donated to the hospital.

When Sebastian came to visit his sister for the first time, he was amazing. I didn't think I could ever love anyone as much as I loved him, but I could. There was plenty of room and love in my heart for all four of our precious children.

We were moved to a side ward overnight to keep monitoring for Group B Strep and the next day we were sent on our way. Very different to our time with Sebastian as everything was out and ready. We took Polly to my grandma's house, and over the next few weeks, we spent a lot of time there with my mum and aunty as they cleared the house. Polly reminds me of my grandma in so many ways, especially as she has gotten older – she is full of strong will and character. There are times when I look at her, and her posture or hair looks so similar.

Then there was the time weeks later when Polly was in her car seat, and we were stood at my grandma's final resting place as they buried her ashes and someone was saying a few words from the funeral directors, just as Polly did the poo of doom and it made us all laugh. Our little Polly Peanut Chops.

Polly was a model baby until she turned one, decided she hated going to bed and became the most defiant person on the face of the earth. Having a wilful child is definitely character building. We don't want her to lose that fire in her though, she's bloody ace, and dare I say she is a chip off the old block.

Our family all complete. Definitely, no more babies for us!

Besides this, I had no job. I wasn't employed for the first time ever and I had no idea what I was going to do. I had always worked in Beauty Therapy, but I didn't want to work in a salon anymore, there were no teaching jobs, and I was stuck. What else could I teach? What else could I do that was part-time hours and fit around my family? It felt impossible, and this was a time when I felt I had completely lost my identity. I was proud, and it seemed like the hard work I had put into my career over the years had got me nowhere.

When Polly was seven months old, I started working

at our local college teaching employability skills and very basic levels of ICT- a total contrast from the beauty industry let me tell you. I was still teaching though, which was good and it was 50/50 love/hate. I met some incredible people though and some fantastic friends from that time, it gave me the confidence I needed and came just at the right time. It was so rewarding and incredibly frustrating all at the same time. After persevering for 18 months, I left for the job I am currently in- working in a library. Oh yes, at last! Working in a library and learning resource centre at the college where I met my husband (he still works there) for a whopping 38 weeks a year is not bad going. Although 25 hours work, running a national charity, trying to fit in running, studying and most importantly family life certainly keeps me busy.

Me in 1982

Me and my Brother, Andrew

Me in 1987

Me and
my Brother,
Andrew

Ruth and I
have been
friends
since
1993!

Matt and I on
holiday in Sorrento,
Italy 2010.
Feels like a
different life.

Noel and James
hand and footprints

N&J and
Joel Bear

Sebastian Joel Pearson
born 15th August 2012

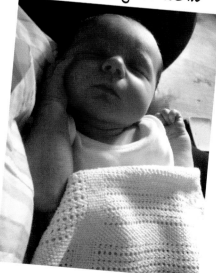

Sebastian bump

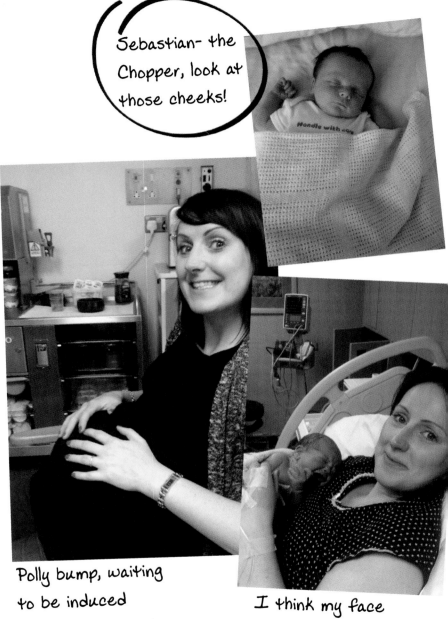

Sebastian- the Chopper, look at those cheeks!

Polly bump, waiting to be induced before being sent home

I think my face says it all! Polly is screaming!

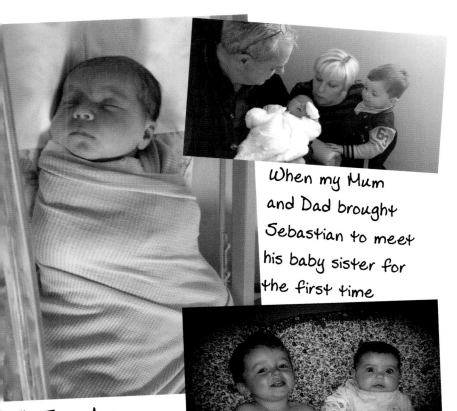

When my Mum and Dad brought Sebastian to meet his baby sister for the first time

Polly Jane Ann Pearson born 2nd May 2014

Sebastian and Polly, full of mischief

Balloons released for Noel and James

Running the Retford
half marathon with
my Brother Andrew
and friend Callie

One of many annoying
pre-run selfies of Callie
and I

The Family Suite after
its full renovation at
Bassetlaw District
Hospital, Worksop

The end is in sight!
Running down The Mall in
the final stretch of the
London Marathon

This photo is the reason I wanted to write a book
about my story. This photo was taken 6 years to
the day when we discovered Noel and James has
died. I had spent all day crying and dreading going
out, but we did it and had a fantastic night with
my two best friends, Ruth and Callie. From mine
and Matts face, you would never know. You never
know what is behind a smile.

With my Mum, Sebastian and Polly before the race for life

Team JOEL at the National Baby Show

Matt and I at the Butterfly Awards as he was nominated as 'Inspirational Father'

Sebastian and Polly with the 'I am a Rainbow' JOEL stickers

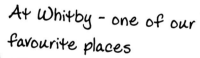

At Whitby - one of our favourite places

Sebastian and Polly's first music festival experience- YNot Festival

Sebastian super excited to watch Manics! First gig

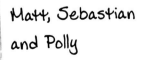

Matt, Sebastian and Polly

Scoundrels

With JOEL Vice
Chair, Sarah at
the Northern
Midwifery
Festival

Polly taking
Joel Bear on
an adventure at
YNot festival

Me with Sebastian and Polly at Rufford Abbey. The place I visited every week after Sebastian was born, with my friend Lisa. JOEL was created on one of these walks.

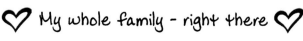

♡ My whole family - right there ♡

But there's one thing I know

The blues they send to meet me

Won't defeat me it won't be long

Till happiness

Steps up to greet me

Hal David- Raindrops Keep Falling on my Head (Manic Street Preachers)

Chapter 6

Head in the sand

Fundraising is a great way to give back. Either a way to give back to a charity or cause that has made a difference to you or in the hope that you could make a small difference to someone else. It offers a welcome distraction to pain and heartache by consuming your life with a never-ending to-do list and getting everyone you know involved it's a win-win situation!

After all, I planned to survive the firsts of everything and keep super-duper busy. Well, fundraising certainly keeps you busy.

After Matt returned to work, about seven weeks after the birth of Noel and James, I spent a lot of time with my lovely dad who is retired and didn't mind me taking residence on his settee and looking after me.

Matt and I had already decided we wanted to organise a fundraising event and I spent time planning this with my dad. We were going to organise a race night and had been offered a venue locally for free, which was a huge bonus. Now, I had never had any experience of fundraising before, but we had been to a few race nights in the past, and they were good fun and looked relatively straightforward to organise (oh how I laugh at this now). We wanted to organise something that was fun and that everyone would enjoy whilst raising funds for two very worthwhile causes.

A month after Noel and James were born, we discovered a local Sands (the Stillbirth and Neonatal Death Society) group in Chesterfield and had been attending their monthly meetings. The support (I'll come to that in a little while) had been incredible, as had that at Bassetlaw Hospital, and therefore we wanted to the money to be split between both.

We wrote letters to every business we knew to donate raffle and auction lots, and the response was overwhelming. We had prizes galore and so many people wanting to support and help us out in our quest. We were gifted the food for the event, so outgoings were zero, and we kept everything crossed that the event would be a huge success. Tickets were a total sell out; we could have sold them twice over. It's such a shame the venue wasn't bigger, but we had managed to squeeze in 100 people, and the ones that came really did mean a lot to us.

The race night took place six months after Noel and James were born and when I was about 18 weeks pregnant with Sebastian. The event was a huge success, and we raised over £3,000 which we split with both our local hospital and Sands group. We requested that the hospital would buy a cold cot for the room known as Room 5, which is where we spent our last hours with our boys. This one evening gave us so much support and hope, as crazy as that sounds. Our family and friends helped us then, and now they were helping us raise funds and awareness, in particular of a wonderful local support group. We couldn't have asked for anything more. As you can imagine, the whole event was emotional. A week or so prior, Matt, my brother, and one of our friends had run a 10k in memory of our boys to kickstart the fundraising, and cheering them on with my little bump made me feel so proud. Dads/partners and other male family members are so often forgotten in all this.

I certainly underestimated the effect fundraising has on your life. It's consuming on every level; physically chasing about everywhere, time spent, the resources needed and the constant to-do list. Generally, the first fundraiser you organise will be a huge success, especially in light of tragic events. People want to support you but don't always know how, so the idea of attending your fundraiser and making a donation is a really good way to do this. It's easy to be fooled into thinking it will be this easy again. Subsequent fundraisers don't necessarily have the same attendance and raise the same funds, plus you will have probably worked even harder to keep the event on its feet. You constantly feel you are asking the same people for money or time and that can become more and more difficult.

After the birth of Sebastian, 'JOEL' was founded, and we decided to raise funds for our new charity and with the shift slightly changed it made a huge impact on our fundraising. As we weren't raising funds for a hospital unit or a registered charity anymore, the donations virtually came to a standstill – the registered charity number gives you integrity and professionalism, and it's understandable organisations do not want to donate to a new 'charity' without any credentials. Trying to get those credentials without any funds also seemed like an impossibility; ideally, you need a £5,000 annual turnover to become a registered charity and raising that amount of funds without a registered charity number is tricky. If we'd known when we had organised our first fundraiser, that we would eventually be setting up a charity these funds would have made a huge difference. However, we are honest and pride ourselves on our transparency and therefore decided to raise the funds by ourselves – for JOEL – raising awareness along the way and not having to hang on to another cause.

It took two years before we became a registered charity. The first year we slightly missed out on the £5,000 target and we were gutted. When the official registration was completed the following year, we decided to take on our biggest fundraiser yet. The big moment came when two National Citizen Service (NCS) groups in Chesterfield chose JOEL as the charity they wanted to fundraise for. One group raised well over £1,000 and that was the moment our application was sent to the Charity Commission.

A few hours after Noel and James had been born we had been moved to another birth room (Room 5) on the labour ward. Luckily, this room wasn't attached to any other birth rooms and therefore this meant we couldn't hear anyone else giving birth or their babies crying, which would have been pure torture. We are always so grateful they didn't move us to a maternity ward. The room was also located immediately next to the entrance of the maternity ward, which meant when our family and friends came to visit again in the evening they wouldn't have to walk through the ward. It also meant we could escape the next morning without being faced with (rightfully) happy faces, healthy, living babies, and balloons celebrating safe arrivals.

The hospital only contained a total of five birth rooms, it's only small, and this was room number five. A room that served a purpose but was clinical, bleak and had no windows. The en-suite only had a shower as it was used for disabled access and this meant I couldn't have a bath (I could have fainted in a shower with the complications and amount of blood I had lost in labour). My husband Matt slept on a put-up bed next to mine as the sofa bed was broken, and this was the room where we said our final goodbyes.

As soon as JOEL was founded, this was something we dreamed of refurbishing. We had hoped the first funds we raised had been used to purchase a cold cot and by renovating this room, we would be able to give families a space of privacy and to allow them to make precious memories with their baby or babies.

Now we were a registered charity, we could potentially work with the hospital and hopefully gain permission to raise funds for the renovation. I had dreamed for so long about how the room could look and feel, and speaking to many other families who had used the room I booked an appointment at the hospital to make our plea.

One of the only things I hadn't 'conquered' since the

birth of our twins was going back into both rooms at the hospital. We were now blessed with two rainbows and somehow had managed to avoid these rooms, and I had almost forgotten that I would probably have to go back into Room 5 if we wanted to make the transformation.

Walking into both rooms, with one of the amazing midwives who was there at the birth of Noel and James, armed with information about our plan for Room 5, brought me virtually to my knees. I had been so unprepared for how this could make me feel. The smells and sights brought back memories I had somehow hidden unintentionally deep in my subconscious. It blew my mind to have these resurface and being there for such positive reasons gave me a huge amount of closure – for that alone I am so glad I faced my fears.

Stepping into Room 5 with a clear mind rather than the fuzziness and shock of the aftermath of stillbirth, really made me realise how much we wanted this project to be a success. Bereaved families were receiving great care, but the room needed to reflect this; enabling us to take on this project was a humongous step for JOEL and a way to give back and say thank you to our local hospital.

So, let's have a bit of fun!

Can you guess how much a room at a hospital with an en-suite, costs to renovate?

£5,000?

£10,000?

£15,000 (this is what I had anticipated)

Getting a little bit closer?

£35,000!!!!!!! Yes, a whopping £35,000!

Bearing in mind that it had taken us so long to achieve a £5,000 turnover, my hopes and dreams shattered. What on earth were we going to do and how could we achieve this?

Of course, we could do this!

We were going to smash it!

Aaaarrrrgh, but what if we couldn't?

After a couple of meetings, I signed the paperwork to

say that we would raise funds to transform this suite and complete a few bits of enabling-works on the other rooms (such as a disabled access bathroom). We had a specific hospital trust fund account designated solely for the use of this precious project and three years in which to do it.

What an immense amount of pressure. We had been raising funds for a while now, but nothing on this huge scale. Our team of trustees was small (only six) and everyone worked and was either pregnant with rainbow babies and/or parents to living children. Our volunteer network was small, but we were hopeful and positive that this could be achieved. In fact, if I did nothing else in my life, I was determined that I would complete this.

So, the fundraising ideas I had ...

- More race nights (we had done it before, so it was an easier option to get started)

- Bag packing at local supermarkets (we became a charity of the year as a result) – this is backbreaking and consumes a whole weekend – but is a good way to raise money and awareness of your cause if there are enough of you

- Making crafts to sell. Don't ask about the few Santa plates we were going to make – that quickly turned into 200!

- Writing funding bids and pleas galore to everyone and anyone. If you haven't completed these before, they take so much time and effort to do properly. They are absolutely worth it though, but with little experience and knowledge, you can write yourself in a big circle. Sometimes passion can look like waffle on paper if you are not careful

The donations started to come in and once it was out there in the local community that we were raising funds for the local hospital to create a bespoke suite for the labour ward the support was unimaginable. We had organised a steering group of JOEL committee members, families and professionals to meet on a regular basis for updates, and these meetings became more and more regular as the money rocketed up.

People were participating in sponsored cycling events, backpacking, offering tombola and raffle prizes. We were selected as charity of the year for a few local businesses. We, also, organised family fun days, and everything else in-between.

In just 10 months we managed to raise £40,000.

I don't feel like I sat on my settee for the whole of that time – we were out every weekend at events – and evenings were spent planning while days were spent working. I also had two very precious rainbows to spend quality time with, and therefore life became like plate spinning. We were here, there and everywhere. But it wouldn't last forever, and the result would be worth every second.

When I look back now, I seriously have no idea how we did it. We lived and breathed the suite, and it helped me tremendously in terms of keeping my mind occupied.

My life focuses so far after Noel and James were born were:

- Survive

- Get pregnant again

- Survive pregnancy (me and rainbow baby)

- Parent a beautiful rainbow

- Plan to try again

- Try again and become pregnant

- Survive a second rainbow pregnancy (again, me and rainbow baby)

- Turn 'Joel The Complete Package' into a registered charity, raise funds and project manage a huge project at the hospital

- Then what?

Not only did this project take up so much effort fundraising, but the planning and efforts behind it all were emotionally exhausting. Going back up to the hospital for steering group meetings every few weeks and then eventually every week were consuming, and then there were the set-backs which we really could have done without in the midst of it all, but these things are there to keep you focussed and more determined than ever.

Before work even started on the room, a disabled access bathroom had to be created in another suite because we were removing this from Room 5. The observation bay was converted into Birth Room 6 as the hospital couldn't function on four birth rooms whilst the work was being completed. It meant that the observation bay had to be moved next door into the pregnancy assessment unit, and we had to have the old early pregnancy assessment unit stripped and painted for them to move into. Have you kept up? This was all before work could even start in Room 5. Each of these processes took approximately two weeks and eventually, on the 3rd May 2016, work started in our family suite. It was estimated to take between six to eight weeks.

The plan for the room was to make it less clinical, to transform it into a bright and airy space, and also imbue it with as pleasant an atmosphere as possible to bring comfort to families who might have been experiencing the worst time of their lives. There was a kitchen area, a sofa bed, a chair with a foot-stool and most importantly a Moses basket that contained a cuddle cot. The cuddle cot was eventually purchased from our fundraising efforts three years prior. A cuddle cot is used to keep a baby or babies cool, which means that families can spend a lot longer with them. The cold mat is soft and flexible and is covered with a blanket, so you can even hold baby wrapped in it without really noticing. A hot room and lots of warm cuddles mean that time spent making memories is very limited and this invention helps give families the time that they need, whether it be an extra hour or a week.

I really wanted the suite to incorporate the colours of the rainbow and be bright and stimulating. The usual theme seems to be neutral and calm, but we wanted to have a very different approach and look. I remember choosing the bright yellow colour for the main wall and seeing the look on everyone's face; I also remember it looking even brighter when a swatch was painted on the wall, but I knew it would look stunning with the grey furniture we had chosen, and it did. There is a tiny bit of each rainbow colour in the room and a rainbow on the floor as you enter.

The family suite is one of my proudest moments ever, from approaching the hospital thinking they would let us add a lick of paint to brighten it up to then being allowed to rip out the whole room and start again was a dream come true. Even if it was a waste of time and money and the room was to gather dust. Saying that the suite is multipurpose and we have received such amazing feedback from families using the room at the worst time of their lives; from families waiting to be induced, even families giving birth to beautiful and precious rainbow babies.

The grand opening was emotional but amazing. It was held in the Boardroom at the hospital, and we were inundated with people keen to attend who had supported the project from day one. On completion of the family suite renovation, I felt a bit strange; it was closure maybe? It also felt a bit like grief I suppose. Not only was it a huge chapter closed – really I would now no longer have any need to go back to the hospital again (definitely no more babies and no more projects there) – it was also the first time in a few years that I hadn't had a massive focus, and I didn't really like it. This project had been my long-term focus after having Noel and James, and now it had been completed. It's a little like planning your wedding for what feels like forever and then when you come home from honeymoon there is a feeling of, what's next? JOEL was only small by this point, and the family suite had been our main project. We knew that we wanted to continue to support families through pregnancy and parenting after loss, but how, and what would we do now? We didn't want the suite, as incredible as it is, to be our one-hit wonder, and here is where the search began.

This project had completely consumed me, and now it was finished. It was the start of the summer holidays, and fortunately, I worked term-time only so it meant I could enjoy much needed time with my rainbow babies, but I was chomping at the bit to get my teeth stuck into something as anxiety soon rears its very ugly head again.

This process taught me so much. It's important not to put the emphasis on one thing only and make a contingency or plan for long-term goals too. The family suite should have taken three years to fundraise and six months to complete and instead the money was raised and work completed in 18 months, and that was with delays to the work. It also taught me that perhaps I should start looking after myself; let's not have any more big projects for a while, eh?

Six months after the project had been completed we met as a Board of Trustees to plan 2017. We wanted a steady year to re-group, avoid burn out and find our new JOEL feet. We made a plan to concentrate on support, and our new Chasing Rainbows group was created; a group where we meet as a family on the first Saturday of each month. In February half term our plans were scuppered when we discovered that we had been shortlisted for the People's Project, a Big Lottery Fund project. We had applied the previous summer and had been shortlisted to the final eight, but not the final five; that would go to public vote. A couple of weeks before the campaign was due to launch, a charity dropped out, and JOEL was first reserve. We were the only charity competing which was run solely by volunteers!

The People's Project features on ITV and winners receive up to £50k - as if we would win that! It was amazing publicity though and to think that JOEL was going to feature on local prime-time TV was exciting. It was all top secret though, and we had to ask everyone to come along to a 'Chasing Rainbows' session for a special occasion, it was there that we told everyone what was going on. The short video clip captured us all brilliantly, and we planned our campaign on a zero budget, around full-time work and our children and families. We certainly like to set ourselves challenges.

When our 'Rainbow Rocks' campaign launched we had two weeks to win the largest proportion of the public vote, and what two weeks it was. All we had was a couple of banners with our voting link on, a 'Rainbow Rocks' t-shirt each and a ridiculous amount of voting slips and links to vote online. That was it. Oh yeah, and copious amounts of passion and energy. It was totally bonkers!

The campaign ended, and we knew that whatever would be, would be – it was out of our control, and we couldn't have given any more than we had. Rainbow Rocks had been given everything we had, and now we just had to wait for the votes to come in.

A few days later, Matt was at home with Sebastian and Polly, and he phoned me at work saying that the People's Project had been in touch and wanted to meet us in a couple of hours. We were all at work – except for Matt – arrrgh! I virtually begged work to go home for a few hours (an hour's drive away), and I made it to the Golden Ball (home of the JOEL Hub) as fast as I could. A few of us had managed to escape work for an hour, and we sat there nervously waiting for what felt like an eternity. Over the previous few weeks, I had watched many a People's Project video on YouTube for ideas of campaigns and the presentation to the winners, and secretly I thought that this was a good sign. A presenter and cameraman walked in and asked if they could move their car to the Golden Ball carpark (sneaky) and then left. Our hearts were in our mouths as we waited for them to return, only to look out of the window to see them filming!

In they walked with a camera and a huge golden envelope which Matt opened to reveal we had won the £50k! The most surreal moment ever. We were so bloody grateful to everyone who made the effort to vote but also completely knackered. What a year and it was only April. Two years previously we had struggled to raise £5,000 a year to enable us to register as a charity; since then we had raised over £40k for a family suite, and now we had managed to win £50k through our 'Rainbow Rocks' campaign. This is where the work really started though. The 'Rainbow Rocks' funds meant we had a load of resources to develop and a conference to plan. Exciting times but super hard work in the process, oh, and the money all had to be spent in 12 months!

'Rainbow Rocks' allowed JOEL to:

- Produce a Pregnancy after Loss journal

- Create Employer and Employee support resources

- Work on support for Siblings in School resources

- Offer free 'Pregnancy After Loss' stickers for women's maternity notes

- Host our very first conference held at the School of Artisan Food at the Welbeck Estate

- Attend the National Baby Show, Midwifery Festivals, and many more events

- Develop our support networks and charity collaborations

- Plus so much more...

Now the funds have been spent, and the resources have been written, now is the time to promote what we have and take in the unbelievable feedback we have received.

Anger is an energy

Bill O. Laswell / John Lydon, Public Image Limited- Rise

Chapter 7

Funky legging obsessions

Oh, where would I be without running?

I would be very grumpy that is for sure.

If you know me, I am the least sporty and least competitive person ever. In fact, I spent a lot of my life avoiding PE/sport like the plague and the thought of it used to bring me out in hives (just kidding). I have always made an effort to keep fit, and have attended to the gym, but not on a regular basis, and usually only to counteract the fact that I love food and am partial to a glass or two of wine.

In the past, I have attempted running. The furthest I could run was two miles, and I used to set off like the clappers and then feel like I was going to die.

However, after Polly was born, I was fed up with the gym, and thought I'd have another go at running. It was the summer and running is always a great idea on warm summer evenings. I can't quite remember how, but I ended up joining a local running club with the hope that it might spur me on to go a little further. I dreaded going for the first time, but everyone made me feel so welcome, and after a month or two I decided to book onto a 10k race to push myself and give me the incentive I needed to go further.

The thing I have found with running on the street on your own is to try and be discreet - it can be nigh on impossible to look good running unless you are super fit with a thigh gap to die for. Unfortunately for me, I am just over 6 feet tall, and discretion has never really been my friend.

I decided to take the running steady as I have rheumatoid arthritis that can flare up in no time at all and therefore I was a little scared of aggravating my joints. So I figured reaching a 10k once would mean that I had met my goal and could tick it off my list of stepping outside my comfort zone.

I ran the Sheffield 10k with my husband, who made it look like a breeze. It definitely wasn't a breeze to me! But it was the furthest I had ever run, and I was proud of myself. All I wanted to do was to make it round the route without walking, and the running community is so supportive. It really did blow me away. Flippantly, I said that I would set myself the challenge of running 10x10ks the following year in the hope it would get me super fit (hahaha) and raise some money for JOEL.

What I didn't realise was how much I was starting to enjoy running. It wasn't about the time or the distance, but it was about being outside in the fresh air without a care in the world. I could be me again. It was nice to push myself and clear my mind of the million things I was thinking about all day long. I couldn't think of anything else when I was running because these were the only things on my mind:

- Running is ace

- I hate running

- I think I'm going to be sick

- I am not wearing my glasses and can't see a thing

- Why am I doing this?

- I think I'm going to die and would anyone find me?

- Starving...

- Now it's starting to feel good and I can breathe again

- Shall I go a bit further?

- Don't forget to stretch again (and not be able to walk for two days)

As silly as this all sounds, it was better than thinking of my eternal to-do list, and when I did get back home, I felt great. It creates a total sense of achievement. It then starts costing you a fortune as you feel worthy of buying some proper leggings, decent trainers (for my great size 9s!) and entering a load of runs (it's all about collecting those medals and finishers' t-shirts). It's liberating, and I felt very frustrated when I couldn't go, although, in true Emma-style, I put everything else before doing something for myself and would miss out on that special time when my mood was low.

Something else to spur you on is a running partner, someone who is about the same pace as you and will help you pass the time of a longer run. I am lucky that one of my best friends has taken up running and her filthy conversation has been known to make me laugh until I get a stitch but we really do spur each other on, especially in the cold winter months.

Running 10x10ks in a year sounds very do-able, although the cost for you and your husband to take part in a series of runs, plus the impact it has on lots of nice weekends you could spend with your family, can be frustrating. We completed the challenge but vowed never to put that amount of pressure on ourselves again. It's easy to become carried away when you're enjoying something so much and have a huge passion for fundraising, but when the activity that keeps you sane starts to affect your life negatively, it's time to reassess and think how you can go about it differently.

The next year I ran simply because I wanted to, and it was great, but I wasn't pushing myself to go further and would cut short longer runs because I felt like I hadn't the time to do them. I now know that I was lying to myself and feeling guilty for making time, mostly when I felt I could/should have been doing JOEL things, and the guilt that I was attaching to it spoilt my enjoyment of an activity I had grown to love. I put far too much pressure on myself and felt a bit jealous of everyone else who appeared to be leading a care-free life, whilst I was mostly burdening myself with rubbish.

In 2017, everything fell into place in so many different ways, and one of those was running. I had a partner and was going regularly, I was running further than I ever had and it felt really good, plus I felt strong mentally and physically and therefore decided this would be the year to take part in a half marathon. It was also the year that JOEL was successfully given a charity place at the London Marathon, and I had bagged it for myself. I had entered the ballot for the London Marathon for three years (whilst also secretly hoping I wasn't successful) and I hadn't been successful. It's a very weird feeling to not be given a place and experience a 50/50 feeling of disappointment and relief. When JOEL was awarded a place through the Charity Ballot, it was incredible, and to think this was something I was actually, finally going to take part in was overwhelming.

The Worksop Half Marathon was a great place to start and meant that if I could complete it, then I knew I would have a really good chance with the marathon.

A half marathon is 13.2 miles, more than twice the distance of a 10k, and even though we had been running 9 miles easily in training, I was nervous about the day. It just seemed so far. We also knew the route and sometimes I don't think that helps as it can make you feel a little overwhelmed. If you know Worksop at all, a 5-10 minute drive in any direction leads to some beautiful countryside, and Clumber Park is one of my favourite ever places. Luckily the Worksop Half would take us through this stunning park to the lake, and the route is renowned for its stunning views.

I ran with my brother Andrew and running buddy

Callie, and we kept each other going and laughed a lot. We finished in a great time, and my rainbows ran the last 100 yards with us all, which made it even more special. Never in my life did I think I could run this distance. I was always envious of people who had managed it and there we were, running 13.1 miles, with not as much training as we should have. Surely this meant a marathon was possible?

During the race, my right foot started to hurt, right under my big toe and my joint started to swell. For a few days, my foot was hot and sore, and I was adamant that this was the start of my arthritis flaring up. I was gutted, I knew that would be it and my running days were over. Why didn't I listen to my consultant, he always told me not to run. He told me to take up swimming (oh how I hate swimming unless it's to a pool bar ha!) – argh!

Luckily, I had an appointment to see a chiropodist a few days later to sort out my battered feet, and there she discovered a tiny shard of glass stuck in my foot, causing the inflammation, swelling, and infection. It was removed, drained and bandaged. I couldn't run for a week, but my legs ached so badly I wasn't bothered, and I skipped back to my car. Yippee! Problem solved.

Rheumatoid Arthritis is where your body starts to attack the ligaments around certain joints in your body, which can eventually leave them quite disfigured. My body does love to attack itself (I'll not bore you with the rest). It started when Matt and I bought our first house and decorated it from top to bottom as soon as we moved in. I thought the paintbrush had made my wrists ache, and it didn't take much after years of massaging and doing nails. I was also busy at work signing portfolios and marking assignments constantly so that also aggravated it. But it didn't start to settle; it got worse. My feet and knees started to hurt too; I could hardly bend my knees. It got to the point where on one occasion I was laid in bed with one of my arms on top of the duvet, and, as Matt got into bed, the cover moved ever so slightly, and the pain was horrific. I screamed, cried (I'm not a wimp) and probably swore profusely and this resulted in a middle-of-the-night trip to A&E, as surely I had broken my wrist and didn't know.

Both wrists were bandaged, and I had to visit my

GP, who referred me immediately to Rheumatology. Surely only old people got arthritis? I was only 25! My joints were so weak that I couldn't push a door open, turn a handle or turn the key for the ignition of my car – even with two hands. Not ideal for a Beauty Therapist. It took a while to calm with medication, and after six years of taking it, I stopped. Four years in remission of my arthritis with no flare-ups and no medication. Apparently, it won't last longer than seven years and then flare ups will be worse, and harder to control, but we will see. It's always in the back of my mind. I don't run when it's slippy as I am scared of jarring myself and starting a flare up. So, I felt this was my time, and so, my one and only chance to complete a half and potentially a full marathon, and if I didn't grab it with both hands, I would regret it. I figured, especially with our recent history, that anything could happen at any time, and I should keep on going, I wouldn't let my fear stop me.

After the Worksop Half, the three of us booked the Retford Half Marathon for the following March as we enjoyed it so much. Plus it would be great training for the London Marathon in April, did I mention that I was running that...?!

Whoever said running was free was kidding. Races, clothing, accessories, trainers, food... the list goes on. The more you run, the more you want to spend.

Shouting at the world you'll never change
But it's what's inside you've got to rearrange

Andy Cairns, Therapy- Nowhere

Chapter 8

Be crazy and set up a charity

In the midst of our grief over losing Noel and James, we had decided to set up a charity. A legacy for our twins and rainbows and a place where we felt safe and comfortable to celebrate our family as a whole. I can honestly say I never imagined the amount of time and work it would take, let alone the space it fills in your head. There have been so many times I have wanted to give up and pack it all in, so many times where I have actually thought, what am I putting my family through? But that is all completely counteracted by the people and families I have met, the support we have received and the pride I have in my heart.

When you set up a charity, it is important to have a

clear vision of what you want to achieve. It doesn't matter if you are not quite sure how you are going allyto do it, you will find the right path for you if it is meant to be – that is what happened with us at JOEL. It is important to always dream big.

JOEL was an idea my friend Lisa and I had come up with together as we met for our weekly walk around Rufford Abbey with our children. We were both on maternity leave at the same time, and I used to love getting out in the fresh air and having a good natter, it really did help me at such a tough time. Lisa was pregnant when we lost the twins, and I always admire the fact that she offered us so much support when it would have been easy to keep away (in my experience people can sometimes treat you like pregnancy loss is catching, or like they are doing you a favour by spending time with you)

JOEL was founded to fundraise and give back to a local support network and our hospital. As time passed, we realised as a family that we still needed support, but it can be difficult to fit in with existing support groups when your rainbows are there. I didn't want to leave our precious newborn rainbow baby Sebastian to attend an evening meeting, nor did I want my husband to miss out on the opportunity for support. We needed something we could attend together as a family. It was probably less about simply our grief over Noel and James and more about our whole life after loss. The pain and heartache of losing a child never fades, but your life learns to grow and adapt around it. Loss is life-long and expecting people to be 'over it' within a year is bonkers. Grief, or being overwhelmed, can happen at any time, for no apparent reason; you can't turn it on or off – it happens when it needs to. For us, there came a point where our good days lasted longer than our bad days, and I didn't want to be stuck in one sad moment forever. I wanted to talk about all of my children with pride and a smile.

I had met a lady called Claire at our local Sands group. Claire and I decided to set up a playgroup for rainbows at a local Sure Start centre and that's where it all began. We had no funds, no resources, apart from a couple of leaflets and no idea really what to expect. The majority of the time it was just us two with our boys, but it didn't matter. We would natter, be able to talk about whatever we felt like, and we took it from there.

Publicising a group in a small town can be hard and that was probably why it stayed small. Eventually it was 'too small' for a Sure Start group (who would ever want that group to be full?), and therefore, we had to find a new home. We played around with days, times, etc., to try and find a happy medium and eventually we decided to give it a rest and take stock of what we wanted to do. The playgroup had a small closed Facebook group, which meant we could chat on there if we wanted. It only had a few members and seemed very restrictive just having a group for Worksop. After all, the joys of the internet mean you can reach people far and wide at any time of the night and day and this is where our online support started. I know I needed it.

The long days on my own at home with Sebastian when Matt went to work fuelled my feelings of anxiety, something that I think happens a lot with mums, whether you are struggling with grief or not. Babies are amazing, but they don't talk to you, and sometimes you can feel quite isolated and lonely, especially when you are exhausted with sleep deprivation – everything can start to feel irrational. The complications of adding our tragic story to my tales of motherhood meant that I dreaded being asked if this was my first baby, so I shied away from groups for this reason, although I can't say they were my cup of tea anyway. I eventually found an amazing baby signing group which helped keep me sane.

The online group meant you could write however you were feeling – day or night – and generally, there would be someone to reply. I spent so much time on there when I was up with night feeds, telling people who were then strangers how I felt because we had a mutual understanding. The group identified missing areas for support and gave me so many ideas on how to develop JOEL.

Time passed and the groups were still small; we had no experience of marketing and how to reach families who needed our support. We had started to raise funds for the Family Suite at our local hospital, and our local community got behind the charity, not only helping us raise funds within 10 months rather than three years, but they also raised a lot of awareness and knowledge about JOEL, and this proved to be priceless. It gave us opportunities to network and collaborate with others, including local employers, councillors, and voluntary sectors. Networking in a charity could be a full-time job on its own. I love it and thoroughly enjoy meeting and working with others, but it can be difficult at times to fit around work, which leads to so much frustration. In fact, frustration is definitely a keyword in the charity world. This is mostly because you have such high expectations for the charity and you desperately want others to share your vision, but, as with all charity work, it's dependant on volunteers, and people giving up their precious time, which can be tough – no, actually it is tough. The more you do, the more you want to do, and soon enough you are working every night, all weekend and constantly thinking, planning, replying to emails, writing huge to-do lists, folding tombola tickets, supporting other families, the list goes on.

Setting up a charity is also very good for avoiding feelings of anxiety as there is always something else to think about and you allow yourself to become completely consumed by everything but your endless worries. Avoiding natural feelings is not good though, and they soon come back to bite you on the arse, big style, but I shall come to that a little later.

We became a registered charity, which took a while, but this meant that we had been awarded the integrity we had been striving for and a real sense of purpose behind what we wanted to achieve. Completing a constitution and formal policies and procedures which are accountable to the Charity Commission is daunting; trustees are liable for the outcome of the charity, and everything needs to be transparent. The documents blew my mind! Night after night I spent time on the dreaded laptop; the times I dreamt of dropkicking it out the window were many, but it was worth every second, and we had worked so hard to be there. At the time, to register as a charity, the annual turnover had to be a minimum of £5,000, and this sounds realistic, right? Well, if we had sorted this within the year of our mammoth race night, it would have been easy, but we had used the promise of giving the money to another charity and the hospital, and there was no way we would have piggybacked on that to enable us to become a registered charity. Even though it took us a couple of years, I think it shows JOEL has longevity and we are here to stay.

It was a challenge making sure our charitable aims were not too restrictive but also gave a clear identity to the support and services we wanted and hoped to offer. I had a huge vision for JOEL, but I knew there was no way I would have been able to do it on my own – nor would I have wanted to – successful charities are always a team effort. How did we even really know that this is what families wanted? Listening and responding to calls for support from bereaved families reaching out to us has been essential. Over time we have had to change, adapt and evolve into how JOEL is presented today, and we have only been able to do this because of the team and the families we support.

It's so easy to become swept up in your own feelings of loss – how would *I* want to be supported? What do *I* need? – When actually everyone has their *own* unique ways of dealing with things and there is no right and wrong way. The support on offer needs to be inclusive for all and not limiting. Families that come to our groups meet Team JOEL and chat to us, so they know that we will always listen to them, encourage them to try to see the positives, to find hope and most importantly learn to laugh and be happy again.

Raising funds for the hospital after becoming a registered charity raised JOEL's profile within the local community. Worksop is by no means a big town, but the community we live in is so supportive of JOEL and the work we do. When people you have never even met want to help you fundraise and raise awareness of the work you do it is just an incredible feeling.

As it stands, this is JOEL:

- Nine trustees

- Approx. 50 volunteers – although we are always on the lookout for more

- A Hub – office space donated to us by a local church. The Hub is used as an office, distribution centre, meeting room and most importantly a space where families have received counselling, coaching, hypnotherapy and 1:1 support

- A bespoke Family Suite – a converted birth room at Bassetlaw Hospital; we also raised funds to create an additional birth room from an observation bay, plus other works

- A huge range of resources developed in-house to support parents, schools, siblings, employers, grandparents, and professionals

- Attendance at and involvement in a huge range of collaboration with other charity networks and support organisations, exhibitions, events, and meetings

- Running an online shop and now an actual shop within a local business

- Running group support sessions Chasing Rainbows, for families, plus our JOEL Dad's and partners' sessions

- People's Project winners – after an intense campaign we won the public vote and were awarded £50k from the Big Lottery Fund!

We are so proud of the fact that all of this is achieved by volunteers; nobody (yet) is paid to work for JOEL. Many of us have paid employment outside of JOEL, we all have families and other commitments, yet this is what we have managed so far. This is what we have achieved in our 'spare' time. Can you imagine how much we could achieve if we had a team dedicated to JOEL full time? We have always dreamed big, and our vision for the charity is HUGE, and I do think this is so important; you need goals, dreams, something to work towards to be able to grow and support the families who need us most and this also applies to life in general. It's good always to have something to work to towards. My husband loves to hear me banging on about stuff that I say I have always wanted to do – taking on far too much and too many things going off already – and this is why our relationship works so well... I definitely need reining in at times, ha! But if I don't have anything to work towards or a goal, then I just struggle to function.

Too much pressure, this pressure got to stop
Too much pressure, it's getting to my head

Neol Davies, The Selector- Too Much Pressure

Chapter 9

The struggle is VERY real

As I have outlined previously, I have to work towards something continually; if I don't have a target, a goal and a dream that I am working towards then I am just hung out on a limb not knowing what to do with myself. I have always worked better in a panic-induced pressurised environment, and if there isn't a deadline, then I procrastinate forever. I think this has become worse since losing Noel and James, but I can't remember what life was life before so I don't know if this is what I use as a coping mechanism but sometimes it's just not the best way to deal with things. Sometimes I make my life so unbelievably busy that I can't breathe and I'm completely overwhelmed. I used to look at others and wish I could make more time for myself, sit with my feet up and watch a film (actually sit still for over an hour, gasp!). It made me feel slightly envious. Even though my being busy *all the time* was totally self-inflicted I knew that whenever my life wasn't ridiculously busy, I would get bored, or worse, and fast.

Plus, there is always more. It's hard to find the right balance of being busy whilst also caring for yourself at the same time; it has taken me a long time to learn how to step back and appreciate my life. I love being busy, and that is great, as long as it's manageable, and that is the key.

You can only bury your emotions for so long before they burst out and bite you, big style. I've always been quite an open book, but sometimes when you spend so much time helping and supporting others, you don't share anything about yourself. Now don't get me wrong, I don't want to spend lots of time talking about myself, but there have been times whilst running the charity that have made me feel a bit lonely on the support front (not anymore, thankfully), and not always having somewhere to go myself. I felt like I had to be mindful of and be strong for others, without sometimes considering myself.

Continuing at this pace, plus a never-ending workload with my job and responsibilities at home was starting to make me feel both physically and mentally exhausted. I spent every day feeling frustrated or completely overwhelmed, but I just kept going and thinking of other things to plan or occupy my mind. I am a terrible comfort eater (emotional eating galore), and it was easy to drink a glass or two of wine each night and just get a takeaway because I couldn't be bothered to cook – ironic really as I still managed to cook for my children.

Looking back, I honestly think I had postnatal depression after having Sebastian, possibly also some form of PTSD due to the shock I'd experienced at the time of Noel and James' death, and I was still getting my head around actually giving birth to a live baby after convincing myself that it was impossible. Maybe this should have been picked up, or I could have received help sooner, perhaps this is what the role of a Health Visitor should be, but apparently even after two miscarriages and the stillbirth of our twins, I was only worth one visit from my Health Visitor. One! Better support than I had for Polly though as we didn't receive a single visit. Shocking.

I just wasn't happy, but I felt I should be. I have an amazing family, brilliant friends, a house, a job, a charity that I was proud of, but I wasn't happy with me. Nothing was ever enough, and when you set ridiculous standards for yourself, then you are just destined to fail. I worked part-time but used to cram the days I had off so fully, that I dreaded them coming and used to want to cancel everything. If I had nothing booked though I would hate it, and I'd still manage to waste a day chasing things about but never actually complete anything.   I think that is another key to volunteering; it's so easy to start a job but not actually finish it – whether that is because it's late at night, your children have woken up from a nap, or you are just too tired to concentrate. The never-ending to-do list of stuff that can never be completed or even added to the list in the first place is depressing, hugely depressing, but I felt as though I had to keep going and eventually something would get better. I would surely be able to snap myself out of it? My thoughts and my mind were just filled with negativity no matter how hard I tried for them not to be.

Every day felt the same and usually consisted of:

- Waking up feeling exhausted

- Feeling total dread for the day ahead (even if it was something fun; there was always something I wanted to cancel or not do)

- Spending most of the day eating total crap and drinking far too much coffee because I felt so tired, this made my blood sugar levels go all over the place and in turn mean that I always felt like I had a headache/ migraine

- Rushing about all over the place, not being able to concentrate, procrastinating and achieving nothing

- Always feeling like I had no time

- I wanted to run away; I don't mean leave my family or anything like that, but sometimes I felt so overwhelmed that I either wanted to run as far and as fast as I could or just get in my car and drive until I probably ran out of petrol. Being overwhelmed is claustrophobic and makes you feel trapped

- Not being bothered to prepare or think about food, so just eating whilst in the car or ordering takeaways far too often

- Spending all evening on my phone or laptop

- Going to bed way too late after a couple of glasses of wine to help me 'wind down'

- Not being able to sleep and then disturbed sleep with a gorgeous little three-year-old who liked to get in our bed and fidget every night

- The emotional hangover after speaking, interviews, etc. The day after an event you can feel flat, down and just shattered

Wake up and the next day was the same, and the same, and the same again.

I missed reading so badly as that was always my escape, but my attention span was about three seconds long so I couldn't get back into it anymore. This made me feel so sad.

Eventually, it became so bad that I couldn't hide it anymore, even though I probably wasn't hiding it in the first place. I met with a friend one afternoon and started talking to them about things that were going on and that I was finding really hard at that time – things that I felt like I couldn't talk to anyone about – but this person saw it too, and for the first time I felt as though I wasn't going mad and the relief was immense. Just as we had started to chat, I had to dash off as I was picking my children up from school and about two minutes into my car journey I started to feel really weird. I knew what it was though, as I had experienced the dreaded panic attacks before, but this one felt like the worst I had ever felt. I was taking deep breaths in the car, trying to call my husband in the hope that a familiar voice would bring me back to reality and help me be slightly more rational. He was at work and didn't hear his phone ringing, which made me call him more and panic further.

When I pulled up at school, I got out the car, and I could walk, but I couldn't feel my legs. I was holding onto the walls and fences trying to pull myself up the hill towards the school, and I was sobbing. God knows what I looked like. I felt as though I was going to be sick and die all at the same time. In the space of about two minutes, I had convinced myself that I was going to have a heart attack and croak it on the way to pick my children up from school. Just when it was looking like it was never going to get better, Matt phoned me and calmed me down. Hearing a familiar voice and one that wasn't judging and making me feel daft was exactly what I needed. I picked Sebastian and Polly up from school, hopefully not looking as bad as I felt, I drove straight over to my mum and dad's and stayed there until Matt came home from work.

The accumulation of my grief, anxiety, overworking, plus loads of other stuff that was going off at that time which was not great, took me back to a place where I just wanted to hide under a duvet again, and there was no way that was going to happen. This was the kick up the arse and huge reality check that I needed to start to sort myself out. You can't help and support people if you really need it yourself but continually ignore that need, and you certainly can't appreciate your life when you feel like rubbish. I realised that now was the time to do something about it. I had already started to get back into running again, but I had found every excuse not to go or cut the runs short, and I knew I needed to do something else.

I had thought about counselling; it's a route that seems most common, but I couldn't see what benefit it would have for me. I wanted to be able to look to the future and be more positive; I just couldn't see how counselling would give me that. We had a lovely lady called Charlotte volunteering with JOEL who was a qualified hypnotherapist, and I messaged her for some advice. I actually felt guilty asking for support for myself – really guilty – in fact, I didn't even feel as though I deserved it. I can't believe I felt so bad and now I look back on that time, I feel quite mad at myself for not seeing it sooner and doing something about it.

I booked myself in for hypnotherapy, and it was one of the best decisions I have ever made. The relief was so overwhelming, and, after the course of sessions, my panic attacks had completely vanished and my mind felt a million times clearer and positive. I listen to hypnosis recordings each night as I fall to sleep and I get the best night's sleep ever. I learnt techniques such as thought stopping which prevents me from going down a spiral of negative thoughts but most importantly it has made me cherish my life even more and be able to enjoy it more than ever. In fact, it gave me the courage to believe I could do anything, even write a book!

If you believe in yourself, you can achieve anything. As soon as you start to think negative thoughts, they prevent you from fulfilling your full potential. I was told if something makes you feel good take it as medicine. If you have to take medicine every day to make you feel better, then so be it. This was my cue to start running again –and properly – after all, I had training for the London Marathon to do and it couldn't have fallen at a better time. I had to learn to make time for myself, and I deserved it; there was no more feeling guilty.

Even now, when I become overwhelmed, I use the techniques and strategies I learnt and developed, and I am so pleased that I have learnt above all how to recognise my warning signs for burnout and why it's important to look after myself. No one can do it for you; you have to do it for yourself. You have to be the person to make changes and learn to be kind to yourself. Affirmations are perfect for this. Saying something to yourself which is 100% positive (it must be positive, not "I will not feel anxious anymore" – it needs to be something like "I absolutely deserve to be happy") and you will feel better about yourself almost instantly. All this happened less than a year ago, and I have resolved to never go back to feeling that way again.

Here is what has happened to me since then:

- Not a single panic attack – hurrah

- Two half marathons and the London Marathon (don't worry, there is a full chapter on that!)

- Started reading again

- Lost weight – not intentionally but it just happened with a few changes to my lifestyle and the running. When I look at photos of myself on holiday previously, I was mortified how I looked like I had just let myself go in so many different ways. I had wasted so much time thinking about dieting and eating crap after having Polly that now I try and be healthier and have some balance.

- Felt the happiest and most comfortable I have ever been with myself; I know that I can't and won't be able to please everyone, and I don't want to. *I* need to be happy, and being happy makes me a better Mummy, wife, friend, and everything else that matters to the people who care

- Being able to spot a narcissist a mile away and sticking the rods up

- Starting writing a book, something I had wanted to do my whole life

My life still felt challenging, but mostly I realised I was making it ridiculously hard for myself and blaming everything else. I felt envious of people who seemed to have an easier life – but who says they have? I have everything I have ever wanted, and for that, I feel the luckiest person ever, and now I appreciate it. Sometimes, you just need someone to guide you and help you clear the mist.

How I made changes:

- Who is important? You! Make time for yourself, even if it is just 5 or 10 minutes every day. If you have a hobby that you love and that makes you feel great, then do it. Prancing around the house with my children makes us all feel happy

- Write a gratitude diary. Every night, before I go to bed, I write 10 things I am grateful for from the day. At first, you write the same things as how can you not be grateful for a beautiful family, a roof over your head and food on the table. After a while you start to look at the small things and, even on a bad day, there is so much to be happy and grateful for. I do this before bed as it makes me go to sleep thinking of the positives in my life

- We have started to try and have a day each

week (sometimes it's just too hard so it's a morning/afternoon) where we spend time as a family, just us, and please ourselves. We could go out or sit in the house, watching films in our pyjamas – it doesn't have to be anything elaborate or expensive

• Get plenty of sleep, eat well, try to be outside for 15 minutes a day and banish the laptop/phone/tablet an hour before sleep. Again, I have wasted far too much of life on an evening looking at what someone who I went to school with nearly 20 years ago (I know I don't look that old, ha) had for their tea

• Friends, and quality over quantity every time. Who cares if you have one or 20, as long as they are people you want to spend time with, and they make you laugh. This last few years has made me realise who my friends are and as we all get older and go through testing times, you find out who is genuinely your friend. If anyone can put up with me talking absolute crap (or my dancing!) on a night out after a drink.... or four... then they are a keeper

- Be more active. No one ever feels better without fresh air and a bit of exercise (unless you physically can't) – blow those cobwebs away

Nothing is perfect, you can never be 'fixed', but who would want to be. Our lives and experiences have made us who we are, and people should be celebrated for surviving the shittiest times of their lives, not be made to feel as though they have to hide away. Hypnotherapy didn't fix me, but it changed my life for the better, and for that I am grateful.

And you may say to yourself,

"My God! What have I done?"

Brian Eno / Christopher Frantz / David Byrne / Jerry Harrison / Tina

Weymouth, Talking Heads- Once in a Lifetime

Chapter 10

This toenail's gone to heaven

If someone had said to me five years ago that I would enjoy running, I think I would have just laughed hysterically, never mind the prospect of taking part in the London Marathon. I can just imagine the shock on my PE teachers' faces from school, ha! The only pair of trainers I owned for years were Converse and are they even technically trainers? Okay, compared to my beloved para boots or New Rocks they were about as trainer-ish as I could possibly do. The only running I did at school was cross-country, and that was only to a place where I would be hidden with a couple of friends, going twos up on a ciggie (sorry mum!) then waiting for everyone to start running back and then follow them. I hated PE; hated being picked last in any team, hated the school showers (cruelty)! How hilarious that my husband is super sporty and was a Sports Lecturer at college when we met.

After three years of unsuccessful ballot entries (the type of unsuccessful where you want to do it but are kind of glad that you're not successful all at the same time), someone mentioned that a charity could also apply for a ballot place too. So there I was filling out another ballot place for me and one for JOEL. It was September when we were told that JOEL was successful and I had planned to take the first charity place unless I was given one in the individual ballot and then I would pass my place onto someone else. No one was given a ballot place, which meant I would be running on my own. The furthest I had even run by this point was 10k, slowly, and even the prospect of a half marathon seemed too far out of my league. I had plenty of time to train though and booked on my first half marathon in Worksop in October 2017.

Now even a half marathon seemed well out of my league, but you can't knock a trier, and after only running 10 miles once in training, I was looking forward to it. I ran (slowly) with my brother and one of my best friends, and I felt like I was holding them back, but we did it together, and the achievement was incredible. It took 2 hours and 35 minutes, which I was more than happy with.

My training for the marathon ticked over until the New Year, and then the horrendous weather started. It felt like the worst winter EVER. Every time I ran it was freezing, snowing, icy, sleet, the list goes on. It never ended. Although, making myself go and run and fit in training was making me enjoy it. I ran a lot on my own, listening to music for the first few miles until I got into it (I always hate the first three miles!) and then I would enjoy the time and peace on my own for the first time in years. I was starting to love it and was so grateful to have something to train for. In March 2018 I had booked onto another half marathon in a local town called Retford with my brother and a couple of friends, and it really boosted my confidence. It was the first time I took part in a run, and I enjoyed it. I knocked 25 minutes off the time of my first half marathon, so I was super happy.

The training (and the snow) continued. It even snowed at Easter. My runs were getting longer, and my friend would join me for the second half to keep me going; sometimes by the time she joined me I had seriously had enough and she had to give me a right good talking to; other times it was brilliant. I ran 20 miles and came back feeling amazing.

Two weeks before the marathon I had started to taper my runs to prevent tiredness and injury and looked at people running on the streets with envy. What was happening to me? The butterflies also started, and the nerves/excitement crept in; I was so excited but absolutely bricking it all at the same time. Everyone knew I was doing it and I was incredibly lucky to have fabulous support and sponsorship, but I was so scared that I wouldn't finish and let everyone down. Deep down, it may come as a surprise, but I am actually quite shy. Clearly, I am a good actress.

On the Thursday before the big day, I travelled down to London on my own to visit the Expo at the Excel and collect my race number. The Expo is just a huge exhibition for the London Marathon where you can buy anything and everything related to the event. You have to go there to collect your number and timing chip by the Saturday, or you are not allowed to take part. Visiting this event was surreal – am I actually doing this? What was more surreal was the fact that it had gone from a freezing winter with snow, to what felt like tropical conditions, in the space of about two days. It was scorchio, which would be great, but not whilst I was attempting the furthest distance I had ever run, please.

My husband Matt, running partner Callie, and I travelled down to London on the Saturday, and it was very strange going away for the weekend without a few cheeky drinks on the train. We would be away for two nights which was the longest I had ever been away from Sebastian and Polly. Even though I knew they were in the best hands possible (stopping with my mum and dad), I missed them as soon as we left. Even though Sebastian told me on many occasions that he could run it twice in the time it would take me as he was the fastest ever – he was probably right. He did also make me promise that he could run it with me when he grew up, and I really hope that happens.

We arrived in London, had a walk to Soho, where we had dinner - pizza of course then made a pledge to go to bed early as we would be up at 5.30am. The most sensible I have ever been in my life! I actually slept, and at 6am we went for breakfast, which consisted of porridge, toast, and bananas. I felt sick! Everyone around me looked like professionals, and I was just hoping to get round in one piece. It was already starting to feel hot, and emails from the organisers kept coming through to let everyone know it would be the hottest marathon on record and how to look after yourself. The hottest temperature I had trained in was probably around 6 degrees and the weather for the day was forecast at 25, oh joy.

We set off to Greenwich with our mascot JOEL Bear and 26 very precious medals; each one was a mile dedicated in memory of a baby or babies. Mile 26 was dedicated to Noel and James, not only because they were born at 26 weeks but because I was running in their memory and in honour of their younger siblings. I had to get to mile 26 even if I had to crawl it. I had already had a good cry on the tube, listening to the reasons why people had chosen to run, mostly in memory of a loved one, and I proudly told them my story too.

We reached Greenwich at 8.30am, and the sky was bright blue with not a cloud to be seen. It was already hot so I decided to run in a cap (which I hated!) just so I could tip water on it to keep me cool. I left Matt and Callie and went into the runners' areas on my own and spent the majority of it in a queue for the toilets. The dread of needing a wee when running and having to queue for hours was not appealing and in fact, worried many people in the wonderful London Marathon Training 2018 #lmt2018 group that I was in. Why I worried about that, I have no idea. In fact, everything I was worried about was trivial and a way of avoiding the fact that I was about to run 26.2 miles.

I don't know what time I put down on my application, but I was given Pen 8 to start in, and this is the final pen – filled with mascots. I made my way to the front of the pen, but then started chatting with a couple of ladies, then realised we had ended up near the back – crikey! It took 50 minutes in the blazing sun to even cross the start line, and all my nerves had almost completely disappeared by that time. I was super excited and just wanted to get on with it, but the weather and the heat were slightly scary. I was used to running in temperatures about 20 degrees below what it was that day and only a few weeks previously it had been snowing. I was fearful about getting dehydrated or over drinking, and there were loads of health warnings emailed out from the organisers. It was officially the hottest ever London marathon!

As soon as I started running lots of people started walking and it was quite difficult to get through the crowds. As a result, my first mile was paced at five whole minutes longer than I usually run and I am not great at picking up my pace once I have set off. My initial plan was to run for as long and as fast as possible before I got too hot. Before the mini-heatwave, I had planned to complete with a time that started with 4 hours and now I knew there was no chance. I can actually walk faster with a four and five year old than I ran that first mile.

The crowds and other runners were amazing, especially as many of those watching must have been standing there for so long by the time I ran past. Matt and Callie were meeting me at Mile 6, and I could not wait to see them. I saw the 6-mile mark, and I knew they wouldn't be far away, but I just couldn't see them, and I was gutted. I was just getting my phone out of my bag to call them when I saw them both on the embankment looking for me; my tracker was about 100 yards behind where I actually was. I shouted them until they saw me and I was so happy. It gave me the boost I needed and kept me going. The next thing I hear is a familiar voice shouting, "Go on bird", and Matt and Callie were running with me. It was so funny, they ran for a little while and then realised they were now in the fenced area and couldn't get out. I left them trying to climb over the barriers... right next to the police!

When I felt too hot to run, I would walk a little and then set off again. I hate walk/running; I know some people like it, but it makes my legs feel awful. Walking was uncomfortable, and the heat was horrendous. I was meant to be on the lookout for Matt and Callie again from Mile 10, but they couldn't get there and instead had settled for a spot near the 35k mark. Everywhere was so congested and crossing roads was virtually impossible. As I ran towards London

Bridge, I called Sebastian and Polly to show them where I was and that I was halfway. Sebastian is fascinated by London after a school project on the Great Fire; he asked many times if we could go for the day and to see if we could find any 'burnt shops', bless him.

From halfway, I was just plodding. I would run and then when it got too much I would walk for a little. It was so congested with people walking it was hard to get past and seeing so many people laid flat out on the floor, being sick, or with medics was not a good sight. There were a few points where I thought to myself, why on earth am I doing this? Then I would remember and have a little cry or give myself a good talking to. Bizarrely, even though there were lots of people around me, I felt as if I was on my own, and wish I'd had had someone to experience it all with me so we could support each other. My mouth was so dry, and many of the water stations had run out of water; as a result, I didn't have a drink for a few miles. People in the crowd had brought loads of drinks for the runners. Some even held a hosepipe over their garden wall soaking everyone which was amazing. Two fire stations also had their water hoses on, and as I ran through one of them, I saw the most beautiful rainbow.

At Mile 17, a woman handed me an ice lolly, and I don't know how I didn't stop to give her a kiss. It was the best thing I had ever eaten. At the 30k mark (randomly there was a mixture of km and mile markers) my friend Lucy and some of her family were waiting, and I caught a glimpse of their fabulous JOEL banner as I approached. I was so happy to see her, and when I ran to her for a sweaty cuddle, she started crying (hopefully not because I was properly stinky) and told me she loved me and that was it, as I ran off I just burst out crying (I have a delightful photo of this moment from one of the official photographers). I was absolutely exhausted by the heat and felt like I had forever to go.

I knew I had the 35k mark to look forward to though as Matt and Callie would be there waiting and by the time I reached them it had cooled just slightly, and I was back on it. I was determined to run to the end, and my legs and feet felt good when I was running. Running down the Embankment, about two miles before the finish, I started with a horrific stitch that I couldn't shift and every time I ran I felt as though I was winded. I was so mad at myself; I was so close! My Garmin had packed up so I had no idea what my time was and I just kept trying to run. The last mile and the crowds were unbelievable; everyone felt very emotional coming to the end, and I couldn't wait to finish and eat something that wasn't a jelly baby. I saw the sign that says 385 yards to go and Buckingham Palace, and that was it, I was off like a whippet. Okay, maybe not quite, but I sprinted down The Mall as fast as my legs would take me. As I crossed the finish line, I had a good cry in front of the poor lady who gave me my medal.

I bloody did it!!!!!!!!!!!

Boom!

I wandered around delirious and seriously in need of a bag of ready salted crisps (the food that fixes everything) and went to collect my bag. I put on my flip-flops, ate a few snacks and then received a phone call from Matt to say they couldn't cross over the road and reach the meeting point, so I had to go and find them. At this point I was sat on a kerb, not knowing how on earth I was meant to stand again, but somehow I did. I walked, very similar in gait to that of a Thunderbird, all the way back up to near Big Ben and then we got in a taxi back to the hotel as I was well and truly spent.

When we arrived back at the hotel, I phoned my parents and spoke to my precious little rainbows, and I so wished they were with me to give them a huge cuddle.

We went for a meal, although I wasn't really hungry. I didn't even have a celebratory drink. I just wanted a hot bath and to lie on a bed and not move again. Although moving the next morning was very interesting.

Running a marathon is a bit like childbirth; you spend months preparing for it and you know it's approaching but no one can actually prepare you for the day. There are times where you feel like you have nothing else to give, but you keep going, and the sense of achievement is unbelievable. It was one of the best days of my life, and I would do it all again in a heartbeat. Anyway, my finish time was 6 hours 1 minute and 2 seconds. Totally gutted it started with a 6 (there are those ridiculously high standards making me feel like a failure again!) and therefore a marathon and I have unfinished business!

If this world makes you crazy
And you've taken all you can bear
You call me up
Because you know I'll be there

Billy Steinberg and Tom Kelly- True Colors (Cyndi Lauper)

Chapter 11

Support

Over the years the JOEL group has grown in so many ways, and the number of people affected by loss is too much to bear sometimes, however, what people are prepared to do for others, even if they have never actually met, is just breathtaking. We all have different lives, different experiences, but the same ache in our hearts.

After Noel and James were born, we left the hospital with a memory box and an over-photocopied Sands leaflet. It was so over-photocopied that you couldn't tell if the people on the leaflet were male/female had eyes, lips or anything. We just put it to one side as it didn't inspire us to find out more and left it at that.

The twins were born in September and Baby Loss Awareness week is in October, just one month later. On the 15th of October, the International Wave of Light takes place, and this is where you can light a candle in memory of babies taken too soon at 7pm and let it burn for one hour. As this event is international, it means a candle is burning somewhere in the world for a whole 24 hours, and it's a beautiful time for families to reflect or support each other.

Good old social media meant that just at this time, someone was sharing some information on their Facebook page about a Sands group in Chesterfield, probably about 16 miles away from where we lived. Sands that rang a bell. It made me dig out that terrible leaflet and read it again and then search Facebook for this new Sands group based close to where we lived. Surely these groups couldn't exist because stillbirth just didn't happen in 2011? How wrong was I? I found it and messaged the page; we had survived a month after the loss of our boys with the support of our midwife and a friend who had lost a daughter many years ago – we were grateful for their support, but we still felt so alone.

We received a lovely message back from Nicky, the lady who ran the group, and we were invited to their next support group, which still runs on the first Tuesday of each month. The group hadn't been going for long, so there were only a few families attending, but sadly this grew and grew over the ten months that we attended. It took a lot to walk into that room, like, every bit of strength we had, but we did it, and I am so glad we did. We met friends there that will last a lifetime and to be able to understand how others felt and for them to understand us was just overwhelming – comforting and heartbreaking all at the same time. It was there that I met Claire, who has been Secretary at JOEL since day one. She was a few months further into her journey than us and pregnant again – OMG! People tried again? I thought it was just us that wanted to. Every month I used to ask her question after question about trying to conceive and pregnancy, it gave us so much hope. Claire's eldest rainbow, Noah, was born a few months before Sebastian and seeing someone have a baby after loss made us feel it was slightly possible because when you are pregnant again, it can feel impossible.

The support we received at the group was amazing, but after Sebastian was born in August 2012, I couldn't go back. Even though it was 11 months after Noel and James were born, I couldn't leave Sebastian, and I felt guilty for going and being happy with my new rainbow baby when others had just started their journey of loss.

Our midwife for Noel and James, and subsequently Sebastian and Polly, was fantastic. She never gave up on us and made us feel as though we could ask anything and drop in constantly for a little listen in on the Doppler. She was matter-of-fact and but had empathy, and that's what mattered. I remember going back into the hospital when I was pregnant with Sebastian and the midwives being so happy to see us and saying they had been hoping we would be back soon. To think people are rallying around you is amazing. People really do live and breathe your rainbow pregnancy with you as they also desperately want everything to be okay.

When JOEL was founded we decided that we wanted to offer support that was different, and we used our knowledge and experience of the existing support to try and do something slightly different. There is no point in re-inventing the wheel. If something works, let them do it; we knew we wanted to try and have a new approach.

Our online closed support group started as a result of the playgroups in Worksop and then in Mansfield. The small groups were designed to allow chats after meeting at the groups but the more time I spent online, I realised that there were so many families across the UK and internationally that were not receiving the support they needed through pregnancy and parenting after loss. We decided to change the group and offer it out to any families that wanted to join, not just locally. And this support group has been my lifeline; as soon as I discovered I was pregnant again with Polly the support I received was unbelievable. It's so hard to explain how you can open up to people who you have never met and develop such a strong trust relationship online.

The online group also means that we really can follow a journey after loss – through trying to conceive, pregnancy and parenting after loss. The hope and support on offer for people who have never met each other (and some who might never meet either) are amazing. The times I've seen someone say they are struggling or are going to have to go to the hospital on their own and the number of people who have jumped up and offered to go along without being asked, or even knowing that person, is so special. This group has also allowed me to be part of a community that feels safe and non-judgmental; it has enabled me to make some strong bonds with a couple of people in particular that I couldn't be without. One lady, I have known a few years but not met until recently, and that was just incredible. Online support means you can type when you can't speak. You can share things you can't always bring yourself actually to say. It means you can spend three days writing a post that you want to share to delete it then because you now feel completely different to how you did when you started writing it. I have done this so many times, and I thought I was the only one.

Support comes in so many different forms, and it doesn't always have to be someone who understands exactly how you are feeling. Many of us go through times that are difficult and incredibly challenging or completely devastating. It's not the situation or experience that you share in common but your outlook, your ability to deal with things in a similar way to others. It's about listening and not comparing, as we all know there is nothing worse than baring your heart and soul only to be told that a friend of a friend's work colleague also lost a baby, but she had another and is okay now. It's like we have to feel as though we have an understanding, an answer for someone else's suffering, even if you don't, even if you can't possibly hope to ever truly 'get it', even if you wanted to (and why would you)? Just listen, don't judge, don't offer 'solutions', and simply be there when someone needs you. Whether it is a month, a year or a decade later the grief *never* goes away, and it never shrinks in size, you just learn to live your life around it.

You also need support for your whole family as it is important to know what to say to children in particular. After Sebastian was born, and then Polly, we have also been determined to tell them both about their big brothers born before them. They do know all about them, although you can never anticipate the questions that come along when you least expect it. Explaining death, not just any death, but that of their older siblings who died inside their mummy's tummy is enough to blow anyone's mind, let alone a child's.

Then you become a bit worried about explaining death because you feel that they are too young to know about the shit life can throw at you. My rainbows ask questions at the most bizarre times ever. I remember driving to gymnastics and Sebastian asking why Noel and James died and why they couldn't stay. Fighting back the tears, I prepared myself to explain and answer all his questions, but just at that moment he saw a plane flying overhead ("Look at that plane Mummy!") and that was the end of that. Totally distracted and not bothered about carrying on the conversation. But then I think of how my parents must have told *me* about death. I had always known about members of my family who'd died before I was born, my Grandad being one of them. Yet with that, I have never been frightened of it, so they must have done a pretty good job of explaining. Open and honest and no fluffy terms such as 'fell asleep'.

Things that are said to offer support but that supposedly can mean nothing:

- Everything happens for a reason. *Just remind me what reason that would be again?* I have always been a big believer in fate (I'm an old romantic at heart), and this was meant to be my life. I was meant to meet and make the most incredible friends who feel like family. I was meant to found JOEL and all that it has become. But I don't want to be told that everything happens for a reason because sometimes the reason is just that life can be shit.

- At least you can get pregnant – *cheers for that*

- At least you can have another – *how do you know?*

- Some things just weren't meant to be – *such comfort*

- I understand how you feel; I was heartbroken when my dog died a couple of years ago – *yes, I can appreciate that must be shit, but really? Comparing the death of a baby to the death of a pet is just never helpful or appropriate.*

Things that *have* helped me:

- When people say: "Tell me about Noel and James"

- A good hug – I have always been a tactile person and a big hug when I feel crap is a winner, especially ones when I don't have to say anything really. I must just look like I need one

- When people aren't dismissive of your feelings

- Talking to others who listen and never judge – if you are one of these people who are capable of just listening, you are a total legend

- Honesty

The amount of messages and emails we received

from friends and family desperately wanting to support and help someone that they know and love is just wonderful. Being part of a charity never fails to let me see the true kindness and thoughtfulness of people, it's lovely. In fact, the care and support we have received over the years has just been awesome.

Within Team JOEL, we all support each other and are mindful that many have times of the year that are tough for us all. Birthdays/anniversaries are difficult, Christmas can be awful, plus the dreaded year that should be our children starting school. We look after and nurture each other, after all, we are doing this out of love, because we have a passion for helping and supporting others and because we care. It's the best team I could ever wish to be a part of; now more than ever, it really is the best. We are there for each other, and when you are working hard to run a charity in your spare time, this is important. We've had stalls at the National Baby Show, Midwifery Festivals, charity balls and so many other different events.

If you listen to stories and share your own that can be emotionally draining. I have been part of many interviews on the radio as our local radio has been a fantastic support, but even though it may not come across that way, they always take their toll emotionally as they can bring all the grief bubbling up to the surface again. Our trustees also are prone to a little mischief, and I do think you have to be able to have this balance when you are part of a National Charity, you can't and don't need to be the face of JOEL 24 hours a day. For example, my now lovely friend and vice chair Sarah bought far too many bottles of fizz at an incredible charity ball held in Manchester and attended by many a Coronation Street and Hollyoaks actor. However, I don't think anyone could have been prepared for my dancing or should I say galloping around the dance floor with a multi-coloured rainbow bear (our JOEL Bear mascot). We are just normal, everyday people. (Okay, maybe just slightly nuts!)

When you throw yourselves, as a team, into environments that are not only amazing but sometimes tough, it's important to have good people around you and make sure you take some time out when needed, and this applies to anything in life.

If people can't see things are getting too much, you need to tell them.

I could deny

but I'll never realise

I've been Chasing Rainbows

all my life

Alan Steven Leach / Paul Adrian Banks / Richard James Witter /

Thomas Peter Gladwin, Shed Seven- Chasing Rainbows

Chapter 12

Be the best version of me

It has taken me 36 years to feel completely comfortable and confident as me. This is not a reflection on anyone else but me, although, I do think that when you hit 30, you really start to care less about what other people think about you and also your perceptions about yourself. Would I be happier if I was thinner or earned more money? No, probably not. Chasing after stuff that we think makes us happy can make us forget what *truly* makes us happy. The more stuff we have, the more we want, and that is not good for anyone; it can make you feel as though you have not accomplished anything. Yes, I would love to be fitter and healthier but only because I want to be a role model for my children and that is not about how you look but how you feel.

Getting to a point in your life where you feel comfortable with yourself is pretty good, but it doesn't mean you have to stand still and let things slip. You have to do what makes *you* healthy and happy – both physically and mentally – and I have found that surrounding myself with my family, friends, JOEL – and, of course, running – I can achieve the balance that I need. Life is not about being blissfully content every single day, and social media has a lot to answer for in that respect. The number of times I've felt like crap in the past and spent all day crying and then posted a picture on Facebook or Instagram looking happy and without a care in the world because just at that moment I felt okay and was too concerned with putting on a brave face.

A perfect example of this is an occasion in 2017, the anniversary of the date that we discovered Noel and James had died. This date is worse than their actual birthday – there is nothing good about this day – and, because of this, when I saw tickets to go and watch a band on that date with Matt and my friends Callie and Ruth it seemed like a plan to keep us occupied and have something to look forward to.

For two weeks before, I tried to think of every excuse under the sun not to go. I spoke to Matt about it, and as we chatted, I decided to drive rather than have a couple of drinks as I knew that the anxiety of going out would probably mean that I would take Dutch courage to a whole new level.

I cried all day, re-living in my head the moments that had happened six years previously, and I felt sick. The kids came home from school, Matt came home from work, and we got ready. Sebastian and Polly went on a sleepover at their grandparents, and off we went, going out on the worst day of the year, and do you know what? I loved it, and it was the best thing I could have done that day. We were with friends we completely trusted and knew, and they made me laugh – a lot! We took a picture of the four of us together, but that picture does not show the secret behind my smile of the day I had experienced and what that day meant to Matt and I. Never judge a book by its cover. Don't presume people are strong and can handle stuff because you never know what goes on behind closed doors.

Being on a journey of loss, anxiety, pregnancy, and

parenting has been a roller-coaster, to say the least, but I am fortunate to have the people who have joined me along the way for the ride and the things that I have learned have made me the person I am today. I am proud of who I have become. I wouldn't have become who I am today without the things that have happened along the way, and for that, I feel fortunate something good has come out of something utterly devastating.

Becoming the best version of me means that I need to live my life ruled by my heart and not by my head and the negative things that can live in there at times. Living your life doing what you think you *should* be doing rather than how you truly want to can make you feel miserable. By this I mean the things you *can* control, not the things you can't. It takes small steps, but small steps put together over time can make huge changes.

- **Try to surround yourself with positivity** – the gentle, encouraging, non-judgemental kind. Not easy when you're prone to be a cup half-empty person like me. If you can think and be positive, then others around you will start to feel the same. It makes you feel better and suppresses those horrendous negative thoughts

- **Thought stopping.** How many times I have had a thought that has taken me down a path of sheer negativity and misery. Usually at 2am when I am thinking of retaliation to a comment someone made to me about five years previously. What is the point? It's a waste of hours of my life. I was introduced to thought stopping, and it has helped me loads. Snap a band on your wrist (not too hard) to bring you out of the thought and say something 100% positive about yourself, an affirmation. It can make you feel a million times better, and you get quicker at bringing yourself out of the depths of negativity

- **Hypnotherapy and meditation** – amazeballs! Coaching can be pretty life-changing too. The idea is that you are left feeling empowered and incredible because that's exactly what you are!

- **Follow your heart** – if you don't, what's the point? Be happy (which for me means not overwhelming myself time and time again)

- **Surround yourself with people who genuinely care** about you and those who bring out the best in you (and vice versa); life is too short for shit 'mates'

- **You can't look after others if you need looking after yourself.** By that I mean what example am I setting my children if I always put myself last? I don't want them to see that and think it's the norm

- **Get your priorities right** and look after you, now!

- **Be grateful.** Every day I think about the things I am grateful for. My whole life has led me to this point, and I am so grateful for the opportunities I have had to do stuff that I would never have dreamt of having the courage to do (like writing a book, hurrah!)

It also means to recognise those signs and symptoms again, a dreaded relapse, something that I needed to add to this book. You have to still work at life, you can't be 'fixed', and things aren't easy. We all have a limit.

I am writing this because near to the end of writing this book, this is what happened to me. I started to feel shit again, like laughing was an effort, like I didn't want to go out. I felt overwhelmed and wanted to bury my head in the sand. Why? Because I had taken feeling better for granted and stopped doing the things that made me feel good about being me. I think I have run 5k no more than five times since completing the marathon three months ago. I started writing humongous to-do-lists that couldn't actually be completed. I stopped listening to my hypnotherapy before bed and I stopped filling out a gratitude diary. Not all at once, but they just slipped bit by bit without me even noticing at first. Writing is very cathartic, I love it, but the thought of lots of lovely people reading a book all about me and thinking it was crap was making me feel nervous; how silly? Writing the above list of things that make me feel better has made me realise what I need to keep up with and take care of - my mind and heart.

Anyway, at least I know now what I need to do, and today is the day that I give myself the kick up the arse that I need. Tonight, even though it's red hot, I am going for a run. I actually cannot wait. I am going to surround myself with all things positive and look forward to the fact that we only have one more alarm before school is out for the summer holidays. Today I woke up and felt more positive and that is good; tiredness plays a massive part in all of this. The negativity soon creeps in when I feel super tired or just ready for a break.

The best version of me will never be perfect and definitely won't be 'normal'... who wants to be normal anyway? Not me, that's for sure. We all have things in life that change us and make us who we are; it's all about embracing what you can't change.

We can be heroes just for one day

David Bowie- Heroes

Chapter 13

Inspire

Who has inspired you?

I feel lucky that I have met loads of people that inspire me, all for different reasons. I love listening to music, and that also inspires me, you can't beat blasting out some top tunes and singing at the top of your voice to make you feel better (maybe even a cheeky dance too?).

People that inspire me don't have to do anything extraordinary, just be themselves and be getting on with their lives – whatever it has thrown at them. That goes for admiration too.

I have come across so many inspirational people since the start of JOEL, either through meeting families and hearing their stories or connecting with people that give up their precious time to help and support others. What could ever be more inspirational than seeing someone who is struggling themselves help and support someone else? The things I have heard people say and their actions blow me away. Giving people hope, when you feel hope is impossible, is a great gift.

Above all, my family inspires me the most, and why wouldn't it? They keep me bursting with pride and grounded all at the same time, the things I so desperately need. I am definitely not an inspirational person, although if I can be stupid enough to drag myself around 26.2 miles of the London marathon, anyone can, especially in the year of the heatwave. In all seriousness, go for it! Put one foot in front of the other and just keep going

And it looks like we might have made it

Yes, it

Looks like we've made it to the end

Alexander James / David Rowntree / Damon Albarn / Graham Coxon,

Blur- To the End

Chapter 14

The end... for now

So here we are, at the end of my book (chuffing hell, I've only gone and finished it!) and my story so far. It doesn't end here (well, hopefully not, anyway) and who knows what the future will bring. I certainly couldn't have predicted what the last seven years have brought.

On the one hand, I am a bereaved mum and on the other a mum to two precious living children. I am a co-founder and chair of a national charity which is professional and works damn hard, but on the flip side I love a night out, a few too many shots, and a few shocking dance moves. I love going out with my friends and going to gigs because this is what I have always loved doing and this is when I am me, the same me that I have always been but sometimes forget is there.

All I know is as I am writing on this beautiful summer's day, I am waiting to pick two of my beautiful children up from school to spend the next six weeks with them – no doubt driving each other potty and having lots of fun all at the same time. We are taking them to their first festival this weekend and seeing the best band ever (Manic Street Preachers, of course)! I have learned that my heart can be full of love and still ache at the same time. Maybe this isn't *normal*, but this is my life.

With thanks to ...

There are so many people I would like to thank; it is overwhelming how many people have helped and supported us over the last seven years...

Karen Cousins, Julie Douglas and Rachel Simpson, for all your support, love and care in delivering our beautiful boys, Noel and James and for being lucky enough to have Rachel deliver Polly too.

Lyndsey Mackinnon- for being my midwife throughout all our pregnancies and putting up with my crying ha!

Chesterfield sands, in particular, Nicky Whelan and Emma Shepherd. You were there in our darkest depths of grief.

Bassetlaw District General Hospital, for the care we have received, and also for allowing us to completely transform Birth Room 5 into the stunning, multi-purpose family suite, it is today.

Lisa Bramley- for your support and encouragement to set up JOEL and for keeping me sane after

Sebastian was born.

Team JOEL, What a team! What an amazing Board of Trustees. Thank you for keeping me going, all your hard work and for giving me the opportunity to share my story. I am so immensely proud of us all, what we have achieved and our huge vision.

Jamie Partington, for creating my AMAZING book cover.

Gail Powell, for your help and support through publication.

Matt Bates, for creating my fabulous website.

Frankie Brunker, Michaela Greaves, Kath Fowler, Sarah Head, Shirley Gascoyne, Ruth Whitehouse and Callie Seaman, for proofreading, reviewing and generally putting up with my exclamation mark obsession!

Charlotte Spivey, for helping me in so many ways and giving the confidence to write this book.

My best friends Ruth and Callie (also running buddy!) thank you for being there and also for dragging me out, being utterly filthy, a total bad influence and making me laugh until I can't breathe.

My family, you really are the best, and I love you all so much.

My husband, Matt, I seriously have no idea how you put up with me and my whims, but you always keep me grounded and most importantly, make me laugh, Love you.

To everyone who has been there, supported us as a family, supported me, believed in JOEL and played a part in our lives- we are forever grateful. You are the best!

CHARITY AND CONTACT INFORMATION

JOEL The Complete Package

Registered charity 1158908

Support for families through pregnancy and
parenting after baby loss

www.joeltcp.org

info@joeltcp.org

emma@joeltcp.org

Instagram: @joeltcp

Twitter: @tcpjoel

Facebook: Joel the Complete Package